common core
Performance Coach™

(5)

Mathematics

Performance Coach™, Mathematics, Grade 5   312NASE   ISBN-13: 978-1-62362-807-9
Cover Illustration: © Thinkstock

Triumph Learning® 136 Madison Avenue, 7th Floor, New York, NY 10016

CONTENTS

DEAR STUDENT

Welcome to *Performance Coach*!

We made this book to help you strengthen your mathematics skills. These skills are important to have for every subject you study this year, not just Mathematics.

Each lesson in this book has three parts:

GETTING THE IDEA ❶

Review some of the basic concepts and skills you've already learned.

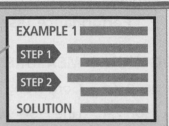

❷ COACHED EXAMPLE

Solve a problem. There are several questions that will help you along the way!

LESSON PRACTICE ❸

Now you're on your own! This part contains more problems to solve.

There are many different types of test items in *Performance Coach*. For some, you will have to choose more than one answer. For others, you will write out your answer. You will also see items that ask you to complete a graph, table, or sentence. Many items have more than one part. Be sure to read the directions carefully so you know how to answer each item.

HAVE A GREAT YEAR!

Sincerely,
TRIUMPH LEARNING

DOMAIN 1

Operations and Algebraic Thinking

LESSON 1

5.OA.2

Writing Numerical Expressions

1 GETTING THE IDEA

A **numerical expression** is an expression that combines numbers and at least one operation (addition, subtraction, multiplication, or division).

$$17 - 11 \qquad 8 \div 4 + 3 \qquad (12 + 7) \times 6$$

You can translate words to numerical expressions and numerical expressions to words.

Example 1

Translate the words *the difference of 12 and 9 divided by 3* into a numerical expression.

Strategy   Look for words that indicate operations.

Step 1   Underline words that represent any of the four operations.

the <u>difference</u> of 12 and 9 <u>divided by</u> 3

Step 2   Translate the meaning of each underlined word to an operation.

The word *difference* means "to subtract."

The words *divided by* mean "to divide."

Step 3   Write a numerical expression for the phrase. Use parentheses if necessary.

$$\underbrace{\text{the difference of 12 and 9}}_{(12 - 9)} \qquad \underbrace{\text{divided by 3}}_{\div\ 3}$$

Use parentheses for the expression $12 - 9$ because the difference of the two numbers is divided by 3.

Solution $(12 - 9) \div 3$ is a numerical expression that represents *the difference of 12 and 9 divided by 3*.

Example 2

Write the numerical expression 12 × (5 + 3) in words.

Strategy Use knowledge of operation symbols to translate the numerical expression.

Step 1 Make a list of words you can use for each symbol or operation in the expression.

×	+
multiply	add
times	plus
multiply by	sum

Step 2 Use words from the list to write the numerical expression.

Examples:

12 times the sum of 5 and 3

add 5 and 3, then multiply by 12

multiply the sum of 5 and 3 by 12

Solution 12 × (5 + 3) can be written as *12 times the sum of 5 and 3.*

Example 3

Which phrase translates the numerical expression 10 ÷ 2 + 8 into words?

10 divided by the sum of 2 and 8

8 more than the quotient of 10 divided by 2

10 and 2 plus 8

Strategy Use reasoning to eliminate phrases.

Step 1 Determine the operations used in the numerical expression and if parentheses were used.

The symbol ÷ represents division. The symbol + represents addition.

There are no parentheses in the expression.

Step 2　Use what you know to eliminate phrases. Then choose the phrase that correctly translates the expression.

~~10 divided by the sum of 2 and 8~~	Eliminate. This phrase would be true if the numerical expression read 10 ÷ (2 + 8). The numerical expression, however, does not use parentheses.
8 more than the quotient of 10 divided by 2	Correct. *8 more* means "add 8." *The quotient of 10 divided by 2* means "divide 10 by 2."
~~10 and 2 plus 8~~	Eliminate. The phrase does not include division.

Solution　The numerical expression 10 ÷ 2 + 8 translates to *8 more than the quotient of 10 divided by 2.*

② COACHED EXAMPLE

Translate the numerical expression (19 − 4) ÷ 5 into words.

Identify the operations in the expression.

The − symbol represents <u>Subtract</u>.

The ÷ symbol represents <u>divide</u>.

Make a list of words that can be used with each symbol.

−	÷
find the difference	distribute equaly

Use words from the list to write the numerical expression.

<u>15÷5</u>

The expression (19 − 4) ÷ 5 can be written as <u>15÷5</u>

1 Circle an operation symbol from each box to translate the phrase into a numerical expression.

9 more than 18 divided by 3

= $18 \div 3 + 9$

2 Angie writes a numerical expression for the following phrase.

10 times the product of 5 and 4

What expression did Angie write?

$5 \times 4 \times 10$

3 Mr. Perez writes the phrase below on the board.

2 more than 15 divided by 3

Determine if the phrase can be translated into each of the numerical expressions. Select Yes or No.

A. $15 \div 3 + 2$ ● Yes   ○ No

B. $(2 + 15) \div 3$ ○ Yes   ● No

C. $15 \div (3 + 2)$ ○ Yes   ● No

D. $2 + (15 \div 3)$ ● Yes   ○ No

4 Write the numerical expression for each phrase. Use the numerical expressions from the box.

Phrase	Numerical Expression
20 minus 2 times 8	$20 - 2 \times 8$
subtract 2 from 20, then multiply by 8	$(20 - 2) \times 8$
28 divided by the sum of 4 and 3	$28 \div (4 + 3)$
3 more than 28 divided by 4	$28 \div 4 + 3$

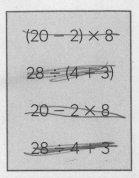

~~(20 − 2) × 8~~

~~28 ÷ (4 + 3)~~

~~20 − 2 × 8~~

~~28 ÷ 4 + 3~~

5 Ramon translated a phrase into the numerical expression shown below.

$$4 \times (30 + 60)$$

Which phrase could he have translated? Circle all that apply.

A. 4 times 30 plus 60

B. 4 times the sum of 30 and 60

C. add 30 and 60, then multiply by 4

D. 60 more than the product of 4 and 30

E. the sum of 30 and 60 times 4

F. add 30 and 60 to 4

6 Translate the numerical expression into words.

$$3 + (45 - 12)$$

three plus thirty three

7 Draw a line from each phrase to its numerical expression.

A. 4 less than the sum of 9 and 2

B. subtract 4 + 2 from 9

C. 9 minus 4 times 2

D. 2 times the difference of 9 and 4

$9 - 4 \times 2$

$(9 - 4) \times 2$

$9 - (4 + 2)$

$(9 + 2) - 4$

8 Translate the numerical expression below into words in three different ways.

24 ÷ 6 − 3

twenty four divided by 3

_____

_____

9 Mrs. Kim asked her students to interpret the numerical expression below.

15 − (7 + 5)

Select True or False for each statement.

A. Add 7 and 5, and then subtract 15. ○ True   False

B. Subtract the sum of 7 and 5 from 15.   True ○ False

C. Subtract 7 from 15, and then add 5. ○ True   False

D. Add 7 and 5, and then subtract the sum from 15.   True   False

10 Eva wrote the words below as a numerical expression in two different ways.

Multiply the quotient of 16 and 2 by 2

Use the tiles to write two different expressions that Eva could have written. Numbers or symbols may be used more than once or not at all.

+	×	÷	2
−	(	)	16

_____

_____

11 Ryan and Isabella translated the words below into a numerical expression.

5 less than the sum of 4 and 6

- Ryan wrote the numerical expression $(4 + 6) - 5$.
- Isabella wrote the numerical expression $5 - 4 + 6$.

Who wrote the numerical expression correctly? RYan

Explain your reasoning.

12 Translate the numerical expression below into words in two different ways.

$10 \times 8 + 9$

_____

_____

Explain why the numerical expression can be translated into words in more than one way.

Evaluating Numerical Expressions

1 GETTING THE IDEA

When you **evaluate** a numerical expression, you find the value of the expression. A numerical expression can contain several types of **grouping symbols**, including parentheses ( ), brackets [ ], and braces { }.

$$\{4 \times [10 \div (2 + 3)] + (20 - 5) \div 3\} - 7$$

Use the **order of operations** to evaluate an expression.

- Perform the operations inside parentheses first, then brackets, and then braces.

- Multiply and divide from left to right.

- Add and subtract from left to right.

Example 1

Evaluate $(8 + 12) \times (6 - 3) \div 2$.

Strategy   Use the order of operations.

Step 1   Perform operations inside of parentheses.

$$(8 + 12) \times (6 - 3) \div 2$$
$$\downarrow \qquad\quad \downarrow$$
$$20 \quad \times \quad 3 \quad \div 2$$

Step 2   Multiply.

$$20 \times 3 \div 2$$
$$\downarrow$$
$$60 \quad \div 2$$

Step 3   Divide.

$$60 \div 2$$
$$\downarrow$$
$$30$$

Solution $(8 + 12) \times (6 - 3) \div 2$ has a value of 30.

Example 2

Evaluate $48 - [(7 + 5) \times 3] \div 4 + 2 \times 11$.

Strategy   Use the order of operations.

Step 1   Perform operations in parentheses.

$$48 - [(\mathbf{7 + 5}) \times 3] \div 4 + 2 \times 11$$
$$\downarrow$$
$$48 - [12 \times 3] \div 4 + 2 \times 11$$

Step 2   Perform operations in brackets.

$$48 - [\mathbf{12 \times 3}] \div 4 + 2 \times 11$$
$$\downarrow$$
$$48 - \mathbf{36} \div 4 + 2 \times 11$$

Step 3   Start from the left side of the numerical expression. Divide first, then multiply.

$$48 - \mathbf{36 \div 4} + \mathbf{2 \times 11}$$
$$\downarrow \qquad\quad \downarrow$$
$$48 - \mathbf{9} \;+\; \mathbf{22}$$

Step 4   Start from the left side of the numerical expression. Subtract first, then add.

$$\mathbf{48 - 9} + 22$$
$$\downarrow$$
$$\mathbf{39} + 22$$
$$\downarrow$$
$$61$$

Solution $48 - [(7 + 5) \times 3] \div 4 + 2 \times 11$ **has a value of 61.**

Example 3

Evaluate $8 + \{3 \times [21 \div (3 + 4)] + 1\}$.

Strategy   Use the order of operations.

Step 1   Perform operations in parentheses.

$$8 + \{3 \times [21 \div (\mathbf{3 + 4})] + 1\}$$
$$\downarrow$$
$$8 + \{3 \times [21 \div \mathbf{7}] + 1\}$$

Step 2   Perform operations in brackets.

$$8 + \{3 \times [21 \div 7] + 1\}$$
$$\downarrow$$
$$8 + \{3 \times 3 + 1\}$$

Step 3   Perform operations in braces. Multiply, then add.

$$8 + \{\mathbf{3 \times 3} + 1\}$$
$$\downarrow$$
$$8 + \{\mathbf{9 + 1}\}$$
$$\downarrow$$
$$8 + 10$$

Step 4   Add.

$$\mathbf{8 + 10}$$
$$\downarrow$$
$$18$$

Solution $8 + \{3 \times [21 \div (3 + 4)] + 1\}$ has a value of 18.

Example 4

Which expression has a value of 12?

$$3 + 12 \times 5 \div (5 + 15)$$

$$18 \div [3 \times (7 - 5)] \times 4$$

$$6 \div 2 \times \{10 + [24 \div (3 + 5)] - 12\}$$

Strategy   Evaluate each numerical expression using the order of operations.

Step 1   Evaluate $3 + 12 \times 5 \div (5 + 15)$.

$$3 + 12 \times 5 \div (5 + 15)$$
$$3 + 12 \times 5 \div 20$$
$$3 + 60 \div 20$$
$$3 + 3$$
$$6$$

Step 2   Evaluate $18 \div [3 \times (7 - 5)] \times 4$.

$18 \div [3 \times (7 - 5)] \times 4$

$18 \div [3 \times 2] \times 4$

$18 \div 6 \times 4$

3×4

12

Step 3   Evaluate $6 \div 2 \times \{10 + [24 \div (3 + 5)] - 12\}$.

$6 \div 2 \times \{10 + [24 \div (3 + 5)] - 12\}$

$6 \div 2 \times \{10 + [24 \div 8] - 12\}$

$6 \div 2 \times \{10 + 3 - 12\}$

$6 \div 2 \times 1$

3×1

3

Solution   The expression $18 \div [3 \times (7 - 5)] \times 4$ has a value of 12.

② COACHED EXAMPLE -

Evaluate $\{4 \times [18 \div (2 + 4)] + (24 - 9) \div 3\} - 7$.

The order of operations for this numerical expression is:

First: perform operations in _____

Second: perform operations in _____

Third: perform operations in _____

Last: _____

$\{4 \times [18 \div (2 + 4)] + (24 - 9) \div 3\} - 7$

_____

_____

_____

_____

_____

The value of $\{4 \times [18 \div (2 + 4)] + (24 - 9) \div 3\} - 7$ is _____.

1 Draw a line from each numerical expression to its value.

A. $(11 - 6) \times 4 \div 2$ •   • 10

B. $(10 + 50) \div (5 - 2)$ •   • 12

C. $14 \div 7 \times (4 + 2)$ •   • 18

D. $25 - [2 \times (18 \div 6) + 1]$ •   • 20

2 Is the value of the numerical expression 45? Select Yes or No.

A. $5 \times (12 - 10) + 7 \times (2 + 3)$ ○ Yes   ○ No

B. $20 + 3 \times [5 + (30 \div 3)]$ ○ Yes   ○ No

C. $10 \div 2 + 5 \times (6 + 2)$ ○ Yes   ○ No

D. $15 - 5 \times 2 + [4 \times (3 + 5) + 8]$ ○ Yes   ○ No

E. $15 \times [13 - (7 + 3) \div 2 - 4]$ ○ Yes   ○ No

3 Circle the numbers and operations so that the value of the numerical expression is 32.

$2 \times$ $12 \div 2 + 4 \times (3 + 5)$

         $12 \div (2 + 4) \times 3 + 5$

         $12 \div (2 + 4) \times (3 + 5)$

4 Write the value for each expression using the numbers in the box. Numbers may be used more than once or not at all.

Expression	Value
$\{[7 + (8 - 3) \times 2] - 5\} + 10$	
$10 + 5 \times [(3 + 21) \div 3]$	
$(8 - 6) \times (3 + 15) \div 3 + 10$	
$2 \times (12 \div 4) + [16 \div (9 - 7)]$	

14
22
50
60

5 Ling wrote a numerical expression that has a value of 18. Select a numerical expression that Ling could have written. Circle all that apply.

   A. $36 \div [7 - (3 + 2)]$

   B. $6 \times (7 + 3) \div 5 - 42 \div (13 - 6)$

   C. $25 \div [(12 - 9) + 2] \times 6 - 3$

   D. $18 - 4 \times (13 - 9) + 16$

   E. $15 \times 2 - 24 \div (11 - 3) - 2 \times 3$

   F. $30 - [(8 - 5) \times 3] + 32 \div 8 - 7$

6 Evaluate the expression below.

$$24 \div [15 - (7 + 2) \div 3 - 4]$$

_____

Describe the steps that you used to evaluate the expression.

7 Juanita evaluated the numerical expression below.

$$4 + 28 \div [2 \times (7 - 5)]$$

She wrote the steps she took to evaluate the numerical expression.
Select True or False for each statement.

   A. Subtract 5 from 7 first.   ○ True   ○ False

   B. Multiply the difference by 2.   ○ True   ○ False

   C. Next, add 4 and 28.   ○ True   ○ False

   D. The value of the expression is 8.   ○ True   ○ False

8 Luke and Andrea evaluated the numerical expression below.

$$(3 + 5) \times 7 - [10 + (45 - 15) \div 5]$$

Luke said that the numerical expression has a value of 48. Andrea said that it has a value of 40. Which student is correct? Describe a possible error that one of the students could have made.

9 Evaluate each expression. Write the expression in the correct box.

$2 \times (8 + 7) - 6 \div 2 \times (9 - 3)$	$20 \div 5 \times (9 - 2) - 2 \times (6 + 3) + 5$

$[25 - 4 \times (3 + 2) \div 5] - 9$	$[(17 - 8) \times 6] \div (2 \times 3) + 6$

12	15

10 Mario ordered new T-shirts for the table tennis team. He bought 6 medium T-shirts and 2 large T-shirts. Each medium T-shirt cost $7 and each large T-shirt cost $9.

Mario received a $4 discount. The final cost of the T-shirts was divided evenly by the 8 members of the team. Write and evaluate a numerical expression to find the amount each team member will pay. Show your work.

Each team member will pay $_____.

11 Hailee placed one set each of parentheses, brackets, and braces in the expression below. The expression has a value of 9.

$$7 \times 20 \div 11 - 9 + 2 \div 8$$

Part A

Write one way that Hailee can place the grouping symbols.

_____

_____

Part B

Explain the strategy you used to place the grouping symbols.

Relating Numerical Expressions

A pattern is a **sequence** of numbers in an ordered list. Each number in the pattern is called a **term**. The first 5 terms of a pattern are shown below.

8, 16, 24, 32, 40, …

You can generate numerical patterns using given rules, identify relationships of the **corresponding terms** between two patterns, and graph the patterns on a **coordinate plane**.

Example 1

Write a rule for each pattern. Then identify the relationship between the two patterns.

4, 8, 12, 16, 20, …

12, 24, 36, 48, 60, …

Strategy Compare terms to identify rules and relationships in the patterns.

Step 1 Identify a rule in each pattern.

Determine what you can do to the first term to get the second term.

Check that the rule applies to every term in the pattern.

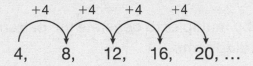

You can add 4 to a term to get the next term. The rule is add 4.

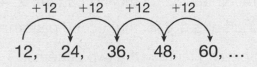

You can add 12 to a term to get the next term. The rule is add 12.

Step 2	Identify corresponding terms in each pattern.

You can list the sets of corresponding terms.

$$\left. \begin{array}{ccccc} 4 & 8 & 12 & 16 & 20 \\ 12 & 24 & 36 & 48 & 60 \end{array} \right\}$$ 4, 12   8, 24   12, 36   16, 48   20, 60

Step 3	Compare corresponding terms.

Compare the terms in the second pattern to the corresponding terms in the first pattern.

12 and 4: 12 is 3 times 4 or 8 more than 4.

24 and 8: 24 is 3 times 8, but not 8 more than 8.

Step 4	Check the remaining terms and identify a relationship.

Terms in the second pattern are 3 times the corresponding terms in the first pattern.

Solution   **The rule is add 4 for the first pattern and add 12 for the second pattern. The terms in the second pattern are 3 times the corresponding terms in the first pattern.**

Example 2

Use the given rules and the starting numbers to generate the first 5 terms in two different numerical patterns. Then identify the relationship between corresponding terms in the patterns.

First pattern: Add 2, starting with 2.

Second pattern: Add 8, starting with 8.

Strategy   **Use counting by multiples to generate the patterns. Then compare the corresponding terms.**

Step 1	Generate the numerical patterns.

Count by multiples of 2 for the first pattern: 2, 4, 6, 8, 10

Count by multiples of 8 for the second pattern: 8, 16, 24, 32, 40

Step 2	List the corresponding terms in the two patterns.

2, 8   4, 16   6, 24   8, 32   10, 40

Step 3 Identify the relationship between corresponding terms.

In the first two corresponding terms, 8 is 4 × 2 and 16 is 4 × 4.

Check each of the corresponding terms to make sure the relationship applies to all of the terms.

The terms in the second pattern are 4 times the corresponding terms in the first pattern.

Solution The two numerical patterns are 2, 4, 6, 8, 10 and 8, 16, 24, 32, 40. The terms in the second pattern are 4 times the corresponding terms in the first pattern.

An **ordered pair** is used to locate a point on the coordinate plane. The ordered pair (2, 5) is located 2 units to the right of the origin and 5 units up. You can make ordered pairs from corresponding terms of two patterns to graph the patterns.

Example 3

The table shows the cost of buying screen-print T-shirts in packs of three.

Number of T-shirts	3	6	9	12	15
Cost ($)	15	30	45	60	75

Identify the relationship between the cost of the T-shirts and the number of T-shirts. Form ordered pairs for the relationship and then graph the relationship on a coordinate plane.

Strategy **Use the numbers in the table to identify the relationship, write ordered pairs, and graph the ordered pairs.**

Step 1 Identify the relationship between the cost of T-shirts and the number of T-shirts.

Identify a relationship between the corresponding terms for the first two terms in the pattern.

15 is 5 times 3 T-shirts. ⎱ The cost of T-shirts in dollars is
30 is 5 times 6 T-shirts. ⎰ 5 times the number of T-shirts.

Check that the remaining terms have the same relationship.

Step 2	Form ordered pairs.
	Write ordered pairs for the corresponding terms in the table: (number of T-shirts, cost).
	The ordered pairs are (3, 15), (6, 30), (9, 45), (12, 60), (15, 75).
Step 3	Graph the ordered pairs on the coordinate plane.
	Plot a point for each of the ordered pairs.
	Draw a line through the points.

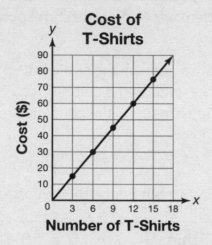

Solution	The relationship between the corresponding terms in the patterns is that the cost in dollars is 5 times the number of T-shirts. The ordered pairs are (3, 15), (6, 30), (9, 45), (12, 60), (15, 75). The graph is shown in Step 3.

The table shows the number of basil leaves and amount of tomato sauce used in a pasta recipe.

Number of Basil Leaves	4	8	12	16	20
Tomato Sauce (in fl oz)	8	16	24	32	40

Identify the relationship between the amount of tomato sauce and the number of basil leaves in the recipe. Form ordered pairs for the relationship, and graph the ordered pairs on the coordinate plane.

Identify a relationship between the corresponding terms for the first two terms in the pattern.

8 fl oz of tomato sauce is _____ times 4 basil leaves.

16 fl oz of tomato sauce is _____ times 8 basil leaves.

The terms in the pattern for tomato sauce are _____ times the corresponding terms in the pattern for basil leaves.

The amount of tomato sauce in fluid ounces is _____ times the number of basil leaves.

Form ordered pairs. (basil leaves, tomato sauce)

The ordered pairs are (____, ____), (____, ____), (____, ____), (____, ____), (____, ____).

Graph the ordered pairs on a coordinate plane.

1 Use each rule and starting number to generate two numerical patterns.

Pattern A: Add 3, starting with 0. _0_ , _3_ , _6_ , _9_ , _12_

Pattern B: Add 18, starting with 0. _0_ , _18_ , _36_ , _54_ , _108_

Identify the relationship between the two patterns.

Something in pattern a x something = something in pattern B.

2 Rami generated two numerical patterns.

5, 10, 15, 20, 25, …

10, 20, 30, 40, 50, …

The rule for the first pattern is _+5_ .

The rule for the second pattern is _+10_ .

Identify the relationship between the two patterns.

_5 x 2 = 10_

3 Mandy made turquoise paint by mixing drops of green tint and blue tint in jars of white paint. The table shows how many drops Mandy used.

Drops of Green Tint	2	4	6	8	10
Drops of Blue Tint	4	8	12	16	20

Circle the rule for each statement.

	add 1			add 2
The rule for green tint is	(add 2)	The rule for blue tint is	(add 4)
	add 4			add 8

Identify the relationship between the two colors of tint.

_2 x 2 = 4_

4 Omar generated two numerical patterns.

10, 20, 30, 40, 50, …

50, 100, 150, 200, 250, …

Which describes the patterns? Circle all that apply.

A. The terms in the second pattern are 5 times the corresponding terms in the first pattern.

B. The terms in the first pattern are one-half the corresponding terms in the second pattern.

C. The rule for the first numerical pattern is add 40.

D. The rule for the first numerical pattern is add 10.

E. The rule for the second numerical pattern is add 50.

F. The rule for the second numerical pattern is add 100.

5 Identify the relationship between the two numerical patterns.

3, 6, 9, 12, 15, …

12, 24, 36, 48, 60, …

_____

6 Select True or False for each statement about the two numerical patterns.

20, 40, 60, 80, 100, …

5, 10, 15, 20, 25, …

A. Add 15 is the rule for the first pattern. ○ True ● False

B. Add 20 is the rule for the first pattern. ● True ○ False

C. Add 5 is the rule for the second pattern. ● True ○ False

D. The terms in the first pattern are 4 times the corresponding terms in the second pattern. ○ True ● False

7 A company sells bags of marbles in sets. Each set contains 2 bags and 40 marbles. Generate two numerical patterns using the rules for the number of bags and the number of marbles in a set. The starting number for each is given.

Number of bags: 2, __4__, __6__, __8__, __10__

Number of marbles: 40 __80__, __120__, __160__, __200__

Write ordered pairs for the two numerical patterns. Graph the ordered pairs on a coordinate plane.

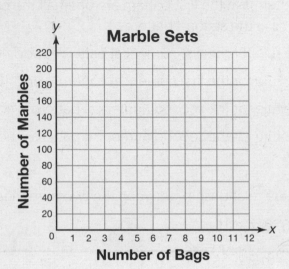

8 Use the numbers in the box to complete the statements about the two number patterns. Numbers may be used once, more than once, or not at all.

25, 50, 75, 100, 125, ...

50, 100, 150, 200, 250, ...

The rule for the first pattern is add __25__.

The rule for the second pattern is add __50__.

The terms in the second pattern are __divide 2__ times the corresponding terms in the first pattern.

2
5
25
50

9 Ed generated two numerical patterns. The rules are add 4, starting with 0 for the first pattern, and add 8, starting with 0 for the second pattern.

0, 4, 8, 12, 16, …

0, 8, 12, 20, 28, …

Did Ed generate correct patterns? Use words or numbers to justify your answer.

NO

10 Look at the two numerical patterns. Select Yes or No for each statement.

15, 30, 45, 60, 75, …

60, 120, 180, 240, 300, …

A. The terms in the second pattern are 2 times the corresponding terms in the first pattern. ○ Yes ● No

B. The terms in the second pattern are 4 times the corresponding terms in the first pattern. ○ Yes ● No

C. The rule for the first pattern is add 15. ● Yes ○ No

D. The rule for the second pattern is add 30. ○ Yes ● No

1 An office supply store sells notebooks in packages of 2. There are 100 total pieces of paper in each package. Generate two numerical patterns using the rules for the number of notebooks and the number of pieces of paper in a package. The starting numbers are given.

Number of notebooks: 2, _4_ , _6_ , _8_ , _10_ , . . .

Number of pieces of paper: 100, _200_ , _300_ , _400_ , _500_ , . . .

What is the relationship between the number of notebooks and the number of pieces of paper? Explain.

notebooks + 2
paper + 100

2 Evaluate each expression. Compare the value to 20. Write each expression in the correct box.

| $(4 \times 5) - 13$ | $6 \times (4 \times 5)$ | $1 + (4 \times 5)$ |

| $22 - (4 \times 5)$ | $(4 \times 5) \div 10$ | $(4 \times 5) + (3 \times 0)$ |

Less than 20	Equal to 20	Greater than 20

3 A museum gives tours to students in groups of 7. Four fifth-grade classes are going to the museum today. There are 20 students in each class, but three students were absent today. The museum needs to determine the number of tour groups. Select True or False for each statement.

A. The expression $(5 \times 20 - 3) \div 7$ can be used to find the number of groups. ◯ True ⬤ False

B. The expression $(4 \times 20 - 3) \div 7$ can be used to find the number of groups. ◯ True ⬤ False

C. There will be 11 tour groups. ⬤ True ◯ False

D. There will be 77 tour groups. ◯ True ⬤ False

4 Jarrod wrote two numerical expressions.

$$100 - 5 \times 2 \qquad (100 - 5) \times 2$$

His expressions use the same numbers and operations. Explain how these expressions are different.

5 Li is 12 years old. Draw a line from each phrase to its numerical expression.

A. Maya is 3 years more than twice Li's age. •

B. Greg is 2 years less than three times Li's age. •

C. Cassie is 3 years less than twice Li's age. •

D. Peter is 2 years more than three times Li's age. •

• $3 \times 12 - 2$

• $2 \times 12 + 3$

• $3 \times 12 + 2$

• $2 \times 12 - 3$

6 The table shows the number of months of cell phone use and the total cost.

Cell Phone Use (in months)	3	6	9	12
Total Cost (in dollars)	$120	$240	$360	$480

Circle the rule to make each statement true.

The rule for cell phone use is
add 1
add 3 .
add 6

The rule for total cost is
add 12
add 117 .
add 120

Identify the relationship between the number of months and the total cost.

_____

7 Kyle and Gia both evaluated the expression $32 \div [8 + (15 - 9) \div 2 + 5]$. Each student's work is shown below.

Kyle's Work	**Gia's Work**
$32 \div [8 + (15 - 9) \div 2 + 5]$	$32 \div [8 + (15 - 9) \div 2 + 5]$
Step 1: $32 \div [8 + 6 \div 2 + 5]$	Step 1: $32 \div [8 + 6 \div 2 + 5]$
Step 2: $32 \div [14 \div 2 + 5]$	Step 2: $32 \div [8 + 3 + 5]$
Step 3: $32 \div [7 + 5]$	Step 3: $32 \div [11 + 5]$
Step 4: $32 \div 12$	Step 4: $32 \div 16$
Step 5: 3	Step 5: 2

Select Yes or No for each statement.

A. Gia correctly completed Step 1. ○ Yes ○ No

B. Kyle correctly completed Step 2. ○ Yes ○ No

C. Gia correctly completed Step 3. ○ Yes ○ No

D. Kyle's answer is correct. ○ Yes ○ No

8 Ella is training for a triathlon. Each week, she will swim 6 more laps than the previous week. Each week, she will run 2 more miles than the previous week.

Part A

Generate two numerical patterns. The starting number for each pattern is given.

Swimming Distance (in laps)	6				
Running Distance (in miles)	2				

Part B

Form ordered pairs to show the relationship between the swimming distance and the running distance. Then graph the pairs on the coordinate plane.

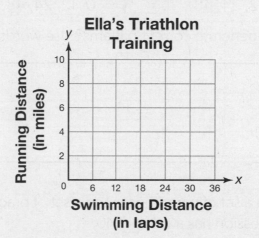

Part C

Identify the relationship between the number of laps and the number of miles.

_____

9 The numerical expression 150 + 4 × 25.75 describes the problem below. Use the numbers from the expression to complete the statements.

Ana started with $_____ in the bank.

She adds $_____ to the account each week.

The expression 150 + 4 × 25.75 represents

the total amount in the bank after _____ weeks.

10 Which expression shows multiplication as the last operation to be performed? Circle all that apply.

A. $(3 \times 9 + 18 \div 6 - 4) \times 3$

B. $(4 + 7) \times (17 - 5) \div 2$

C. $9 \times [(11 - 5) \div 2 + 4]$

D. $18 - 27 \div 3 + (4 \times 5)$

E. $[(6 \times 5) - 22 \div 11 + 3 - 8] \times 10$

F. $15 \div 3 \times 4 - 2 \times 6$

11 Cassie generated two numerical patterns. The rule for the first pattern is add 6. The rule for the second pattern is add 12. Both patterns start with 0.

$0, 6, 12, 24, 48, \ldots$ $0, 12, 24, 48, 96, \ldots$

Did Cassie generate correct patterns? Use words or numbers to justify your answer.

12 Juan added a set of parentheses and a set of brackets in the expression below. Juan's expression has a value of 40.

$15 \div 3 \times 5 + 4 \times 8$

Part A

Write one way that Juan could have written the grouping symbols.

Part B

Explain the strategy you used to place the grouping symbols.

Winter Hats

For your little sister's birthday, you decorated a winter hat to look like a puppy. You did such a good job that 6 of her friends offered you money to make them hats, too! You have enough money saved to cover the cost of the materials needed to make the hats.

Below are the directions you follow to make one hat.

- Start with a ready-made winter hat.
- Cut ears, nose, and mouth from one 12-inch-by-18-inch piece of felt.
- Glue felt ears, nose, mouth, and 2 puppet eyes on the front of the hat.

The table shows the cost of materials.

Material	Cost
Winter hats	$6 for 2
Felt	$1 for each 12-inch-by-18-inch piece
Puppet eyes	$2 each eye

Part A Explain how to find the cost of the materials needed to make one hat. Then write a numerical expression that represents your explanation.

Part B You decide to sell each hat for $12. Rewrite your expression to represent the amount of profit you will make from selling one hat. Evaluate your expression. Show your work.

Part C Use the cost of materials for one hat to complete the table by generating a numerical pattern.

Number of Hats	1	2	3	4	5	6
Cost of Materials ($)						

Write a rule for each numerical pattern in the table. Then identify the relationship between the cost of materials and the number of hats made.

Part D Use the profit made from one hat to complete the table by generating a numerical pattern.

Number of Hats	1	2	3	4	5	6
Profit ($)						

Write a rule for each numerical pattern in the table. Then identify the relationship between the profit and the number of hats made.

Part E You want to continue making and selling hats to earn extra money. To increase your profits, what could you change? Explain your answer.

DOMAIN 2

Number and Operations in Base Ten

Comparing the Values of the Digits of a Number

① GETTING THE IDEA

In the base-ten number system, the values of digits follow place-value patterns. The value of a digit in one place represents 10 times as much as what it represents in the place to its right and $\frac{1}{10}$ of what it represents in the place to its left.

Hundreds	Tens	Ones	.	Tenths	Hundredths
		2			
		0	.	2	
		0	.	0	2

10 times as much as (top to middle) $\frac{1}{10}$ of
10 times as much as (middle to bottom) $\frac{1}{10}$ of

2 is 10 times as much as 0.2.   0.2 is $\frac{1}{10}$ of 2.

0.2 is 10 times as much as 0.02.   0.02 is $\frac{1}{10}$ of 0.2.

Example 1

What is the value of the underlined digit?

36.4<u>5</u>

Strategy   Use a place-value chart to find the value of the underlined digit.

Step 1   Write 36.45 in a place-value chart.

Hundreds	Tens	Ones	.	Tenths	Hundredths
	3	6	.	4	5

Step 2   In which place is the digit 5?

The digit 5 is in the hundredths place.

Step 3   Use place value to find the value of the digit 5.

5 hundredths = 0.05

Solution   The value of 5 in 36.45 is 0.05.

Example 2

Compare the values of the ones and tenths digits in 63.38.

Strategy   Use a place-value pattern to compare the values of the digits.

Step 1   Write 63.38 in a place-value chart.

Hundreds	Tens	Ones	.	Tenths	Hundredths
	6	3	.	3	8

Step 2   Find the values of the ones and tenths digits.

The value of the ones digit is 3 ones, or 3.

The value of the tenths digit is 3 tenths, or 0.3.

Step 3   Use a pattern to compare 3 and 0.3.

The value of 3 in the ones place is 10 times as much as the value of 3 in the place to its right.

So, 3 is 10 times as much as 0.3.

Solution   In 63.38, the value of the ones digit, 3, is 10 times as much as the value of the tenths digit, 0.3.

Example 3

Compare the values of the tens and hundreds digits in 771.52.

Strategy   Use a place-value pattern to compare the values of the digits.

Step 1   Find the values of the tens and hundreds digits in 771.52.

The value of the tens digit is 7 tens, or 70.

The value of the hundreds digit is 7 hundreds, or 700.

Step 2   Use a pattern to compare 70 and 700.

The value of 7 in the tens place is $\frac{1}{10}$ of the value of 7 in the place to its left.

So, 70 is $\frac{1}{10}$ of 700.

Solution   In 771.52, the value of the tens digit, 70, is $\frac{1}{10}$ the value of the hundreds digit, 700.

Compare the values of the tenths and hundredths digits in 449.66.

Write 449.66 in a place-value chart.

Hundreds	Tens	Ones	.	Tenths	Hundredths

Find the values of the tenths and hundredths digits in 449.66.

The value of the tenths digit is _____.

The value of the hundredths digit is _____.

Use a pattern to compare _____ and _____.

The value of _____ in the tenths place is _____ the value of _____ in the place to its right.

In 449.66, the value of the tenths digit, _____, is _____ the value of the hundredths digit, _____.

1 Compare the value of the digits in 5.55. Draw a line from each number to its comparison phrase.

A. 5   •   • is $\frac{1}{10}$ of 5.

B. 0.5 •   • is $\frac{1}{10}$ of 0.5.

C. 0.05 •   • is 10 times as much as 0.5.

2 Evan correctly compared the values of the digits in 477.44. Which comparison could he have made? Circle all that apply.

A. The value of the tens digit is 10 times as much as the value of the ones digit.

B. The value of the hundredths digit is 10 times as much as the value of the tenths digit.

C. The value of the ones digit is $\frac{1}{10}$ of the value of the tens digit.

D. The value of the hundreds digit is 10 times as much as the value of the hundredths digit.

E. The value of the hundredths digit is $\frac{1}{10}$ of the value of the tenths digit.

3 Look at each comparison of the digits in 442.43. Is the comparison correct? Select Yes or No.

A. 400 is 10 times as much as 40.   ○ Yes   ○ No

B. 40 is $\frac{1}{10}$ of 0.4.   ○ Yes   ○ No

C. 40 is 10 times as much as 400.   ○ Yes   ○ No

D. 40 is $\frac{1}{10}$ of 400.   ○ Yes   ○ No

4 Circle one number from each box to make the statements true.

200		0.2			0.2			200
0.02	is $\frac{1}{10}$ of	200	.		200	is 10 times as much as	0.02	.
0.2		20			20			0.2

5 Compare the values of the digits in 99.99. Select True or False for each statement.

A. 0.9 is $\frac{1}{10}$ of 0.09.   ○ True   ○ False

B. 9 is 10 times as much as 0.9.   ○ True   ○ False

C. 0.09 is $\frac{1}{10}$ of 9.   ○ True   ○ False

D. 90 is 10 times as much as 0.9.   ○ True   ○ False

E. 9 is $\frac{1}{10}$ of 90.   ○ True   ○ False

6 Compare the values of the digits in 554.23. Use the tiles to write two different comparisons. Numbers or phrases may be used more than once or not at all.

is 10 times as much	500	0.2	50
is $\frac{1}{10}$ of	5	40	0.03

_____

_____

7 Margo traveled 528.8 miles on her trip. Write a statement that compares the values of the ones and tenths digits.

_____

8 Amir said that the value of 9 in the hundredths place of 135.99 is 10 times as much as the value of 9 in the tenths place. Is Amir's statement correct? Explain why or why not.

9 For each number in the table, write a phrase from the box to complete the comparison.

Number	Phrase
30	
0.3	
300	
0.03	
3	

is 10 times as much as 0.3

is 10 times as much as 30

is $\frac{1}{10}$ of 0.3

is $\frac{1}{10}$ of 3

is $\frac{1}{10}$ of 300

10 Yoshi used the fewest number of bills, dimes, and pennies to pay for a pair of ear buds that cost $14.99. Which is a true statement? Circle all that apply.

A. The number of pennies is $\frac{1}{10}$ the number of dollar bills.

B. The value of the pennies and the value of the dimes is the same.

C. The value of the dimes is 10 times the value of the pennies.

D. The number of dimes and the number of pennies is the same.

E. The value of the pennies is $\frac{1}{10}$ the value of the dimes.

11 Use numbers from the box to complete four different comparison statements about the digits in 642.22.

_____ is $\frac{1}{10}$ of _____.

_____ is $\frac{1}{10}$ of _____.

_____ is 10 times as much as _____.

_____ is 10 times as much as _____.

| 600 |
| 40 |
| 2 |
| 0.2 |
| 0.02 |

12 Will is playing a math game. He needs to use the following clues to write a 5-digit number:

- The number consists of 3 different digits.
- All digits are even numbers greater than zero.
- The value of the ones digit is $\frac{1}{10}$ of the value of the tens digit.
- The value of the tenths digit is 10 times as much as the value of the hundredths digit.
- The sum of the tenths and hundredths digits is equal to the hundreds digit.
- The sum of the tens and ones digits is equal to the tenths digit.

What is the 5-digit number? Use words, numbers, or models to justify your answer.

Multiplying and Dividing by Powers of 10

1 GETTING THE IDEA

Repeated factors, such as $10 \times 10 \times 10 \times 10 \times 10$, can be written using a base and an exponent. A **base** is a number that is multiplied by itself a certain number of times. An **exponent** is a number that tells how many times a given number is used as a factor.

$$10 \times 10 \times 10 \times 10 \times 10 = 10^5 = 100{,}000$$

exponent ↓ ... ↑ base

A **power of 10** is a value represented by multiplying 10 by itself a certain number of times. You can write a power of 10 in exponential form.

Using Multiplication	Exponential Form	Word Form
10	10^1	10 to the first power
10×10	10^2	10 to the second power
$10 \times 10 \times 10$	10^3	10 to the third power
$10 \times 10 \times 10 \times 10$	10^4	10 to the fourth power

You can use a pattern to multiply whole numbers by powers of 10. Write as many zeros after the whole number in the product as the value of the exponent.

$4 \times 10^0 = 4 \times 1 = 4$ **0** zeros

$4 \times 10^1 = 4 \times 10 = 4\mathbf{0}$ **1** zero

$4 \times 10^2 = 4 \times 10 \times 10 = 4\mathbf{00}$ **2** zeros

$4 \times 10^3 = 4 \times 10 \times 10 \times 10 = 4{,}\mathbf{000}$ **3** zeros

Note that 10^0, or 10 to the zero power, is equal to 1.

Example 1

Multiply 0.86 by powers of 10. Explain the pattern that you see.

Strategy   **Look for a pattern.**

Step 1   Multiply by consecutive powers of 10.

$$0.86 \times 10^0 = 0.86 \times 1 = 0.86$$
$$0.86 \times 10^1 = 0.86 \times 10 = 8.6$$
$$0.86 \times 10^2 = 0.86 \times 10 \times 10 = 86$$
$$0.86 \times 10^3 = 0.86 \times 10 \times 10 \times 10 = 860$$

Step 2   Look at the decimal point in each product.

$0.86 \times 10^0 = 0.86$ Decimal point moves **0** places to the right.

$0.86 \times 10^1 = 8.6$ Decimal point moves **1** place to the right.

$0.86 \times 10^2 = 86$ Decimal point moves **2** places to the right.

$0.86 \times 10^3 = 860$ Decimal point moves **3** places to the right.

Step 3   Explain the pattern.

In the product, the number of places the decimal point moves to the right is the same as the value of the exponent. Sometimes you may need to write zeros as placeholders to move the decimal point as many times as needed.

Solution   **When you multiply a decimal by a positive power of 10, the decimal point in the product moves to the right as many places as the value of the exponent.**

Dividing a whole number or a decimal by powers of 10 follows a similar pattern.

Example 2

Divide 0.86 by powers of 10. Explain the pattern that you see.

Strategy   **Look for a pattern.**

Step 1   Divide by consecutive powers of 10.

$$0.86 \div 10^0 = 0.86 \div 1 = 0.86$$
$$0.86 \div 10^1 = 0.86 \div 10 = 0.086$$

$$0.86 \div 10^2 = 0.86 \div 10 \div 10 = 0.0086$$
$$0.86 \div 10^3 = 0.86 \div 10 \div 10 \div 10 = 0.00086$$

Step 2 Look at the decimal point in each quotient.

$0.86 \div 10^0 = 0.86$ Decimal point moves **0** places to the left.

$0.86 \div 10^1 = 0.086$ Decimal point moves **1** place to the left.

$0.86 \div 10^2 = 0.0086$ Decimal point moves **2** places to the left.

$0.86 \div 10^3 = 0.00086$ Decimal point moves **3** places to the left.

Step 3 Explain the pattern.

In the quotient, the number of places the decimal point moves to the left is the same as the value of the exponent. Sometimes you may need to write zeros as placeholders to move the decimal point as many times as needed.

Solution **When you divide a decimal by a power of 10, the decimal point in the quotient moves to the left as many places as the value of the exponent.**

❷ COACHED EXAMPLE

Multiply 4.3 by 10^2. Then divide 4.3 by 10^2.

Compare your results and your work.

To multiply a decimal by 10^2, move the decimal point _____ places to the _____, because the exponent has a value of _____.

To divide a decimal by 10^2, move the decimal point _____ places to the _____, because the exponent has a value of _____.

$4.3 \times 10^2 =$ _____

$4.3 \div 10^2 =$ _____

The product is _____ than the quotient.

To multiply, the decimal point was moved to the _____, increasing the value of the original number.

To divide, it was moved to the _____, decreasing the value of the original number.

1 Select True or False for each equation.

A. $20 \times 10^3 = 2{,}000$ ○ True ○ False

B. $20 \times 10^5 = 2{,}000{,}000$ ○ True ○ False

C. $20 \times 10^1 = 200$ ○ True ○ False

D. $20 \times 10^0 = 1$ ○ True ○ False

2 Circle the number and the word to make the statement true.

To divide 0.92 by 10^3, move the decimal point in 0.92 _____ places to the _____ .

0		left
2		right
3		up
10		down

3 Draw a line from each expression to its value.

A. $2.35 \div 10^3$ •   • 23,500

B. 23.5×10^2 •   • 0.000235

C. $23.5 \div 10^5$ •   • 2,350

D. 2.35×10^4 •   • 0.00235

4 Zach found a rat snake in the woods near his home. Its length is 1.473 meters. Which expression has the value 1.473? Circle all that apply.

A. $0.1473 \div 10^1$ **E.** $14.73 \div 10^1$

B. 1.4730×10^0 **F.** 10.473×10^1

C. $100.473 \div 10^2$ **G.** $147.3 \div 10^2$

D. 0.01473×10^2

5 Circle the power of 10 that makes each equation true.

$$4.63 \div \boxed{\begin{array}{c} 10^2 \\ 10^3 \\ 10^4 \end{array}} = 0.000463 \qquad 0.000463 \times \boxed{\begin{array}{c} 10^2 \\ 10^3 \\ 10^4 \end{array}} = 4.63$$

6 Find the value of each expression. Is its value 21.58? Select Yes or No.

A. $2.158 \div 10^1$ ◯ Yes ◯ No

B. 0.2158×10^2 ◯ Yes ◯ No

C. 21.58×10^0 ◯ Yes ◯ No

D. $215.8 \div 10^1$ ◯ Yes ◯ No

E. $21{,}580 \div 10^4$ ◯ Yes ◯ No

7 Use the numbers from the box to complete the expressions that have the same value as $92.7 \div 10^3$.

_____ × _____

_____ ÷ _____

. _____ × _____

0.00927
0.0927
9.27
10^2
10^1
10^0

8 Compare each expression to 1 whole. Write the expression in the correct box.

0.03×10^4	$0.03 \div 10^1$	$30 \div 10^1$
0.003×10^2	$0.003 \div 10^4$	0.3×10^0

Less than 1	Greater than 1

9 Jen makes beaded jewelry to sell at art fairs. The prices of the bags she can buy are shown in the table below. Jen does **not** want to use beads that cost more than $1 each.

Bag	Number of Beads in 1 Bag	Price of Bag
A	100	$18.25
B	10	$15.50
C	1,000	$12.00

Which bag(s) of beads should Jen buy? Write equations to justify your reasoning.

Bag(s): _____

Equations: _____

_____

_____

10 Select True or False for each equation.

A. $4.17 \times 10^0 = 4.17 \div 10^0$ ○ True ○ False

B. $0.0417 \div 10^3 = 4.170 \times 10^3$ ○ True ○ False

C. $41.7 \div 10^2 = 0.00417 \times 10^2$ ○ True ○ False

D. $0.00417 \times 10^3 = 41.7 \div 10^1$ ○ True ○ False

E. $41,700 \div 10^5 = 0.000417 \times 10^5$ ○ True ○ False

11 Sam is wondering if there is a pattern that he can use to divide the whole number 3 by powers of 10.

Part A

Write a whole number. Then write a decimal equivalent to the whole number with zero tenths and hundredths.

Whole number: _____

Decimal: _____

Part B

Divide the decimal you wrote in Part A by 10^0, 10^1, 10^2, and 10^3. Show your work.

Part C

Is there a pattern Sam can use to divide whole numbers by powers of 10? Explain.

Reading and Writing Decimals

Decimals can be written in different ways, just like whole numbers.

Standard form	25.347
Word form	twenty-five and three hundred forty-seven thousandths
Expanded form	$2 \times 10 + 5 \times 1 + 3 \times \frac{1}{10} + 4 \times \frac{1}{100} + 7 \times \frac{1}{1,000}$

Remember that expanded form is a way of writing a number as a sum of the values of its digits.

You can use place value to help you write a decimal in different ways.

Example 1

The Seikan Tunnel in Japan is the longest underwater tunnel in the world. It is 53.108 kilometers long. Write the word form for 53.108 kilometers.

Strategy   Use a place-value chart.

Step 1   Write the number in a place-value chart.

Hundreds	Tens	Ones	·	Tenths	Hundredths	Thousandths
	5	3	·	1	0	8

Step 2   Write the word form for the whole-number part. Write *and* for the decimal point.

fifty-three and

Step 3   Write the word form for the decimal part. Use the name of the last decimal place to name the decimal.

fifty-three and one hundred eight thousandths

Solution   **The word form for 53.108 kilometers is fifty-three and one hundred eight thousandths kilometers.**

Example 2

Write the standard form and expanded form of two hundred forty-five and thirteen thousandths.

Strategy   Use a place-value chart.

Step 1   Write the decimal in a place-value chart.

    The word *thousandths* tells you that the last digit is in the thousandths place.

    Use a zero as a placeholder for tenths. Use a decimal point for the word *and*.

Hundreds	Tens	Ones	·	Tenths	Hundredths	Thousandths
2	4	5	·	0	1	3

Step 2   Write the value of each digit in the place-value chart.

Hundreds	Tens	Ones	·	Tenths	Hundredths	Thousandths
2	4	5	·	0	1	3
2×100	4×10	5×1		$0 \times \frac{1}{10}$	$1 \times \frac{1}{100}$	$3 \times \frac{1}{1,000}$

Step 3   Write the decimal in expanded form as the sum of the values of the digits.

$$2 \times 100 + 4 \times 10 + 5 \times 1 + 1 \times \frac{1}{100} + 3 \times \frac{1}{1,000}$$

    It is not necessary to write the value of a zero in a number.

Solution   **In standard form, the decimal is 245.013. In expanded form, it is**

$$2 \times 100 + 4 \times 10 + 5 \times 1 + 1 \times \frac{1}{100} + 3 \times \frac{1}{1,000}.$$

Example 3

A number written in expanded form is $3 \times 10 + 8 \times 1 + 9 \times \frac{1}{10} + 2 \times \frac{1}{1,000}$. Which of the following shows the standard form?

    38.92   30.892   38.902   3,892

Strategy   Interpret the expanded form.

Step 1   Determine the value of each addend in the expanded form.

$$3 \times 10 + 8 \times 1 + 9 \times \frac{1}{10} + 2 \times \frac{1}{1,000}$$

    ↑   ↑   ↑   ↑

    3 tens   8 ones   9 tenths   2 thousandths

Step 2   Check if there are any missing place values.

> No hundredths are shown between tenths and thousandths.
> So, there are 0 hundredths.

Step 3   Write the number that has the digits with the same values.

> The number 38.902 has 3 tens, 8 ones, 9 tenths, 0 hundredths, and 2 thousandths.

Solution   The standard form of $3 \times 10 + 8 \times 1 + 9 \times \frac{1}{10} + 2 \times \frac{1}{1,000}$ is 38.902.

② COACHED EXAMPLE

A bakery produced 163.584 kilograms of bread on Monday. Write the word form and expanded form for this number.

First, write the word form for 163.584.

> The word form for the whole-number part is _____.
>
> Write the word _____ for the decimal point.
>
> The last digit in 163.584 is in the _____ place.
>
> So, the word form for the decimal part is _____.

Next, write the expanded form of 163.584.

> Complete the place-value chart.

Hundreds	Tens	Ones	·	Tenths	Hundredths	Thousandths
☐ × 100	☐ × 10	☐ × 1		☐ × $\frac{1}{10}$	☐ × $\frac{1}{100}$	☐ × $\frac{1}{1,000}$

The word form for 163.584 is _____

_____.

The expanded form for 163.584 is _____

_____.

1 Which of the following shows the values of the digits in six hundred three and five hundred eighty-two thousandths? Circle all that apply.

A. $5 \times \frac{1}{10}$ **E.** 3×1

B. 6×100 **F.** 5×100

C. 8×10 **G.** $8 \times \frac{1}{100}$

D. $2 \times \frac{1}{1,000}$ **H.** $6 \times 100,000$

2 The longest snake in captivity has a weight of about three hundred fifty and ninety-four thousandths. Circle the numbers that show the weight of the snake.

35	904
305	409
350	94
355	094

3 Look at each choice. Is it another way to write the decimal 30.425? Select Yes or No.

A. thirty tens and four hundred twenty-five thousandths   ○ Yes   ○ No

B. $3 \times 10 + 4 \times \frac{1}{10} + 2 \times \frac{1}{100} + 5 \times \frac{1}{1,000}$ ○ Yes   ○ No

C. thirty and four hundred twenty-five thousandths   ○ Yes   ○ No

D. $3 \times 1 + 1 \times 1 + 4 \times \frac{1}{10} + 2 \times \frac{1}{100} + 5 \times \frac{1}{1,000}$ ○ Yes   ○ No

4 Determine whether each word form or expanded form represents a 5-digit decimal or a 6-digit decimal. Write the word form or expression in the correct box.

forty-two and six thousandths

$$3 \times 100 + 7 \times 1 + 1 \times \frac{1}{10} + 9 \times \frac{1}{100}$$

one hundred eighty and thirty-two thousandths

$$2 \times 10 + 6 \times 1 + 5 \times \frac{1}{10} + 4 \times \frac{1}{1,000}$$

5-Digit Decimals	6-Digit Decimals

5 Select True or False for each statement.

A. three hundred twenty-four and sixty-eight thousandths is equal to 324.068   ○ True ○ False

B. $596.104 = 5 \times 100 + 9 \times 10 + 6 \times 1 + 4 \times \frac{1}{1,000}$ ○ True ○ False

C. $2 \times 100 + 7 \times 10 + 5 \times 1 + 3 \times \frac{1}{100} + 6 \times \frac{1}{1,000}$ is equal to two hundred seventy-five and 306 thousandths   ○ True ○ False

D. 803.542 is equal to eight hundred three and five hundred forty-two thousandths   ○ True ○ False

6 Kate wrote *nine hundred twenty and forty-seven hundredths* as the word form for 920.047. Is her work correct? Explain why or why not.

```



```

7 Yoshi wrote the standard form for three hundred sixty and nine hundred seven thousandths. Kim wrote a number with 3 more ones and 7 less tenths. What number did Kim write?

Use the place-value chart to help you write the number.

Hundreds	Tens	Ones	·	Tenths	Hundredths	Thousandths

Kim wrote _____.

8 Two decimals contain the digits 0, 1, 2, and 4. Circle the numbers that show the standard forms.

$$4 \times 100 + 1 \times \frac{1}{10} + 2 \times \frac{1}{1,000} =$$
- 0.412
- 400.102
- 4.12

four hundred one and two hundredths is equal to
- 401.02
- 400.12
- 4.102

9 Write the standard form for each decimal.

twenty-six and thirty-four hundredths = _____

$9 \times 10 + 5 \times \frac{1}{10} + 3 \times \frac{1}{100} + 7 \times \frac{1}{1,000}$ = _____

three hundred nine and two hundredths = _____

$1 \times 100 + 7 \times 10 + 8 \times \frac{1}{100} + 4 \times \frac{1}{1,000}$ = _____

10 Dan is writing a report on snowfall in Alaska. Valdez, Alaska, receives an average of 305.8 inches of snow each year. Dan found that this measurement is the same as 776.732 centimeters. Write the number of centimeters in word form.

_____

11 Suzi races on her bicycle. She recorded her times for 3 sprints.

Sprint	Time (in seconds)
1	fifty and five hundred sixty-four thousandths seconds
2	2 hundredths of a second slower than Sprint 1
3	3 tenths of a second faster than Sprint 2

Write the expanded form of each number to explain how to find Suzi's time for the third sprint.

Suzi's time for the third sprint is _____ seconds.

LESSON 7

Comparing Decimals

1 GETTING THE IDEA

You can use place value to compare decimals in the same way you compare whole numbers. You start at the left and compare the digits in the same place-value position until the digits are different.

You can use the comparative symbols below to compare decimals.

Symbol	<	>	=
Meaning	is less than	is greater than	is equal to

Example 1

At a track meet, Javier jumped 19.750 feet in the long jump. Mike jumped 19.625 feet. Compare the lengths of the jumps using >, <, or =. Who jumped the longer distance?

Strategy   **Use a place-value chart.**

Step 1   Write the two distances in a place-value chart.

Hundreds	Tens	Ones	·	Tenths	Hundredths	Thousandths
	1	9	·	7	5	0
	1	9	·	6	2	5

Step 2   Compare the digits in each place-value position until the digits are different.

Start at the left. The tens and ones are the same. The first pair of digits that are different are the tenths.

Hundreds	Tens	Ones	·	Tenths	Hundredths	Thousandths
	1	9	·	**7**	5	0
	1	9	·	**6**	2	5

Step 3	Compare the tenths. Use comparative symbols.

Because 7 tenths > 6 tenths, 19.750 feet > 19.625 feet.

So, 19.750 is greater than 19.625.

Solution   Javier jumped the longer distance.

Example 2

Compare each decimal to 256.109. Write the decimal in the correct box.

256.103	256.901	256.109	25.619

Less than 256.109	Equal to 256.109	Greater than 256.109

Strategy   Use place value to compare each decimal to 256.109.

Step 1	Compare the digits in 256.103 to 256.109 starting at the left.

The thousandths digits are different.

3 thousandths < 9 thousandths, so 256.103 < 256.109.

Step 2	Compare the digits in 256.901 to 256.109 starting at the left.

The tenths digits are different.

9 tenths > 1 tenth, so 256.901 > 256.109.

Step 3	Compare the digits in 256.109 to 256.109 starting at the left.

The digits are the same, so 256.109 = 256.109.

Step 4	Compare the digits in 25.619 to 256.109 starting at the left.

The hundreds digits are different.

0 hundreds < 2 hundreds, so 25.619 < 256.109.

Solution

Less than 256.109	Equal to 256.109	Greater than 256.109
256.103 25.619	256.109	256.901

Which decimal is greater than 543.285? Circle all that apply.

A. 654.328

B. 54.285

C. 543.085

D. 543.298

E. 543.285

For Choice A, compare _____ to 543.285.

Starting at the left, the first digits that are different are in the _____ place.

_____ ◯ _____, so _____ ◯ 543.285.

654.328 is _____ _____ 543.285.

For Choice B, compare _____ to 543.285.

Starting at the left, the first digits that are different are in the _____ place.

_____ ◯ _____, so _____ ◯ 543.285.

54.285 is _____ _____ 543.285.

For Choice C, compare _____ to 543.285.

Starting at the left, the first digits that are different are in the _____ place.

_____ ◯ _____, so _____ ◯ 543.285.

543.085 is _____ _____ 543.285.

For Choice D, compare _____ to 543.285.

Starting at the left, the first digits that are different are in the _____ place.

_____ ◯ _____, so _____ ◯ 543.285.

543.298 is _____ _____ 543.285.

For Choice E, compare _____ to 543.285.

The numbers are _____.

543.285 is _____ _____ 543.285.

The decimals in choices _____ **are greater than 543.285.**

1 Select True or False for each sentence.

A. 85.934 < 85.958   ⊙ True   ○ False

B. 478.711 > 487.711   ○ True   ⊘ False

C. 567.602 < 567.62   ⊘ True   ○ False

D. 84.740 > 84.74   ○ True   ⊘ False

E. 638.35 < 69.403   ○ True   ⊘ False

2 Circle the decimal from each box that makes the sentence true.

38.826			38.826
38.86	< 38.806	38.806 >	38.86
38.086			38.086

3 Isabel correctly compared 805.614 and 805.416. Which statement could she have made when describing her reasoning? Circle all that apply.

A. The first digits that are different are in the thousandths place.

B. All of the digits are the same, so the numbers are equal.

(C.) I compared the digits in the tenths place.

D. I compared the digits in the hundredths place.

E. Because 4 thousandths < 6 thousandths, 805.614 < 805.416.

F. Because 6 tenths > 4 tenths, 805.614 > 805.416.

4 Is the decimal greater than 576.18? Select Yes or No.

A. 575.19   ○ Yes   ⊘ No

B. 576.81   ⊘ Yes   ○ No

C. 576.108   ○ Yes   ⊘ No

D. 576.018   ○ Yes   ⊘ No

E. 579.18   ⊘ Yes   ○ No

F. 576.801   ⊘ Yes   ○ No

5 Compare each decimal to 623.194. Write the decimal in the correct box.

| 623.207 | 623.47 | 623.19 | 622.194 | 624.094 | 623.419 |

Less than 623.194	Greater than 623.194

6 Use digits from the box for each decimal to make the sentence true. Digits may be used more than once.

$972.675 < 972.6\_\_\_$

$972.675 < 972.6\_\_\_ \_\_\_$

$972.675 > 972.6\_\_\_$

$972.675 > 972.6\_\_\_ \_\_\_$

8
2
4
5

7 Justin and Kim each wrote a sentence on the board.

Justin   Kim

$458.308 > 458.38$ $458.308 < 458.38$

Which student is correct? Describe a possible error that one of the students could have made.

8 Write two sentences to compare 743.476 and 743.746.

_____ ◯ _____

_____ ◯ _____

Describe the steps you used to compare the decimals.

```
┌─────────────────────────────────────────────────────────────┐
│                                                             │
│                                                             │
│                                                             │
│                                                             │
│                                                             │
└─────────────────────────────────────────────────────────────┘
```

9 A shipping company charges $40 if the box weighs 28.375 pounds or less. Which package weight can be shipped for $40? Circle all that apply.

A. 28.75 pounds   E. 27.875 pounds

B. 28.025 pounds   F. 283.25 pounds

C. 28.25 pounds   G. 28.5 pounds

D. 29.35 pounds

10 The table shows the speeds of the four fastest drivers in a car race.

Driver	Speed (miles per hour)
Marco	224.362
Finn	224.136
Will	224.48
Liz	224.392

Did Marco win this week's race? Use words, numbers, or models to justify your answer.

```
┌─────────────────────────────────────────────────────────────┐
│                                                             │
│                                                             │
│                                                             │
│                                                             │
└─────────────────────────────────────────────────────────────┘
```

11 Mr. Miller drew a rough map to show how his land is divided into sections. He grows corn, soybeans, and wheat. He also has dairy cows.

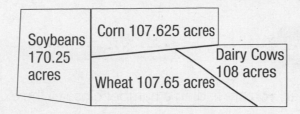

Part A

Write a sentence to compare the number of acres of corn and the number of acres of wheat.

_____ ◯ _____

Part B

Write a sentence to compare the number of acres of soybeans and the number of acres of wheat.

_____ ◯ _____

Part C

Compare each crop area to the land used for the dairy cows. Explain if more or less land is used for each crop than for dairy cows.

LESSON 8

Rounding Decimals

1 GETTING THE IDEA

When you **round** a number, you are finding a number close to the exact number.

To round 9,367 to the nearest thousand, first find the digit in the rounding place. Then look at the digit to the right of the rounding place. Underline that digit.

- If that digit is less than 5, then the digit in the rounding place stays the same. Change the digits to the right to 0s.

- If that digit is 5 or greater, then the digit in the rounding place is increased by 1. Change the digits to the right to 0s.

Thousands	Hundreds	Tens	Ones
9	3	6	7

Because 3 is less than 5, the digit in the thousands place stays the same. So, 9,367 rounded to the nearest thousand is 9,000.

This same process can be used to round decimals.

Example 1

The largest grasshopper in Australia is the Giant Grasshopper. It can grow to a length of 3.457 inches. Round the length of the Giant Grasshopper to the nearest inch.

Strategy Use a place-value chart.

Step 1 Determine to which place you need to round.

   When you round to the nearest inch, you want a whole number measurement. Rounding to the nearest inch means to round to the ones place.

Step 2 Write the number in a place-value chart.

Hundreds	Tens	Ones	.	Tenths	Hundredths	Thousandths
		3	.	4	5	7

Step 3 Find the digit in the rounding place. Underline the digit to the right of the rounding place.

Hundreds	Tens	Ones	.	Tenths	Hundredths	Thousandths
		3	.	<u>4</u>	5	7

Step 4 Look at the underlined digit. Decide what to do with the digit in the rounding place.

Because 4 is less than 5, the digit in the rounding place stays the same. Then change digits to the right to 0s or drop the digits.

3.457 rounded to the nearest whole number is 3.000 or 3.

Solution **The length of the Giant Grasshopper rounded to the nearest inch is 3 inches.**

Example 2

A grasshopper can jump up to 20 times the length of its body. One grasshopper jumped 508.97 centimeters. What is the length of this jump to the nearest tenth of a centimeter?

Strategy Use place value.

Step 1 Find the digit in the rounding place. Underline the digit to the right of the rounding place.

508.9<u>7</u>

Step 2 Look at the underlined digit. Decide what to do with the digit in the rounding place.

Because 7 is greater than 5, increase the digit in the rounding place by 1.

9 tenths + 1 tenth = 10 tenths, or 1 one

Add 1 to the ones digit and change the digits to the right to 0s, or drop the hundredths digit.

508.97 rounded to the nearest tenth is 509.00 or 509.0.

Solution **The length the grasshopper jumped rounded to the nearest tenth of a centimeter is 509.0 centimeters.**

Example 3

Round 39.635 to the nearest tenth and to the nearest hundredth. How do the rounded numbers compare?

Step 1   Round 39.635 to the nearest tenth.

39.6<u>3</u>5   3 < 5, so the tenths digit stays the same.
Drop the digits to the right.

39.635 rounded to the nearest tenth is 39.6.

Step 2   Round 39.635 to the nearest hundredth.

39.63<u>5</u>   The underlined digit is 5, so increase the hundredths digit by 1.
Drop the digit to the right.

39.635 rounded to the nearest hundredth is 39.64.

Step 3   Compare the rounded numbers.

Rounded to the nearest tenth		Rounded to the nearest hundredth
↓		↓
39.6 < 39.635 < **39.64**		

When rounded to the nearest tenth, 39.635 rounds to a lesser number. When rounded to the nearest hundredth, 39.635 rounds to a greater number.

Both numbers are close to 39.635.
39.64 is closer to 39.635 than 39.6 is.

Solution   39.635 rounded to the nearest tenth is 39.6, and 39.635 rounded to the nearest hundredth is 39.64. Rounding to the nearest hundredth results in a number closer to the original number than rounding to the nearest tenth.

Round 18.706 to the nearest whole number and to the nearest hundredth. How do the rounded numbers compare?

Rounding to the nearest whole number is the same as rounding to the _hundredths_ place.

To round 18.706 to the nearest whole number, find the digit in the _hundreths_ place.

Underline the digit in the _hundredths_ place.

_7_ _⊘_ 5, so _7 goes up._

18.706 rounded to the nearest whole number is _19_.

To round 18.706 to the nearest hundredth, find the digit in the _18.800_ place.

Underline the digit in the _thousandths_ place.

_7_ _⊘_ 5, so _number goes up_.

18.706 rounded to the nearest hundredth is _18.800_.

18.706 rounded to the nearest whole number is _19_.

18.706 rounded to the nearest hundredth is _18.800_.

18.706 rounded to the nearest _hundred_ is closer to 18.706 than the number rounded to the nearest _whole_.

1 An elephant at an African wildlife reserve weighed 237.584 pounds at birth. Select True or False for each statement about the weight of the elephant.

A. The weight rounded to the nearest hundredth is 237.58.   ○ True   ○ False

B. The weight rounded to the nearest ten is 240.   ○ True   ● False

C. The weight rounded to the nearest tenth is 237.5.   ○ True   ● False

D. The weight rounded to the nearest hundred is 200.   ● True   ○ False

E. The weight rounded to the nearest pound is 236.   ○ True   ● False

2 Mr. Chin wrote the rounded number below on the board.

82.6

Look at each number. Could it be the number that Mr. Chin started with? Select Yes or No.

A. 82.642   ● Yes   ○ No

B. 82.59   ○ Yes   ○ No

C. 82.507   ○ Yes   ○ No

D. 82.63   ○ Yes   ○ No

E. 81.6   ○ Yes   ○ No

F. 82.553   ○ Yes   ○ No

3 Find what each number in the table could be rounded to. Use numbers from the box. There may be one or two rounded numbers for each number.

Exact Number	Rounded Numbers	
	Rounded Number 1	Rounded Number 2
71.894		
71.955		
72.088		
71.906		

71.9

71.96

72.0

72.1

4 Ethan won a fishing tournament by catching a bass that weighed 10.735 pounds. He wrote an article about it for the school paper. He correctly used a rounded number in the headline. Select a headline he could have used. Circle all that apply.

A. Winning Bass Weighs 10.8 Pounds

B. 11-Pound Bass Caught

C. 10.74-Pound Bass Is Tops

D. Ethan Wins with 11.73-Pound Bass

E. 10.7-Pound Bass Is Biggest Catch of the Day

F. 10.73 Pounds Wins Bass Tournament

5 Circle a place value and number from each box to make each statement true.

62.465 rounded to the nearest

whole number	62.47
tenth	62.4
hundredth	62.46

is .

62.5 is

| 62.564 |
| 62.56 |
| 62.456 |

rounded to the nearest

| whole number |
| tenth |
| hundredth |

.

6 Draw a line from the phrase to a decimal that matches the phrase.

A. 43.582 rounded to the nearest tenth   •   • 43.60

B. 43.528 rounded to the nearest tenth   •   • 43.5

C. 43.585 rounded to the nearest hundredth   •   • 43.6

D. 43.597 rounded to the nearest hundredth   •   • 43.59

7 This diagram shows the heights of some tall mountains in the United States.

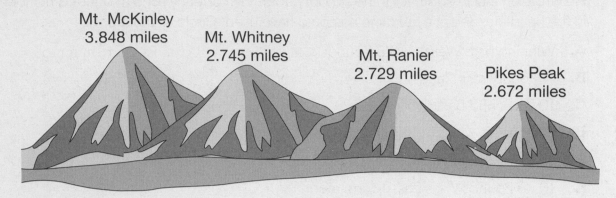

Mt. McKinley
3.848 miles

Mt. Whitney
2.745 miles

Mt. Ranier
2.729 miles

Pikes Peak
2.672 miles

Part A

What happens when you round the heights of each mountain to the nearest mile? Suggest another way to round the heights of the mountains in order to compare them.

Part B

Find two more rounded heights for Mt. Rainier. How do these rounded measures compare to rounded measures of the other three mountains?

8 Two clues in a number game are shown.

- The number has 3 decimal places.

- The number rounded to the nearest hundredth is 84.72.

The least number that matches these clues is _____.

The greatest number that matches these clues is _____.

9 Bahir's science class grew sunflowers for an experiment. The tallest sunflower grew to 2.387 meters. Bahir made a sketch of the sunflower in his notebook. He will label its height with a rounded decimal that will make the sunflower appear as tall as possible.

Should Bahir use a decimal rounded to the nearest meter, nearest tenth meter, or nearest hundredth meter? Explain your reasoning.

10 Ellie is a runner. She keeps track of winning times for women's long-distance races. The table shows the winning times that Ellie found for the women's 10,000-meter race in four Olympic games.

Olympic Results
Women's 10,000 Meters

Year	Time (in minutes)
2012	30.346
2008	29.911
2004	30.406
2000	30.292

Suppose Ellie rounds each time to the nearest tenth. In which two years would the winning times appear to be the same? Explain.

Multiplying Whole Numbers

 GETTING THE IDEA

You can use place value to help you multiply multi-digit whole numbers. A **product** is the result when you multiply two or more **factors**.

Example 1

One of the largest soccer stadiums in the world is in Brazil. There are 78,838 seats in the Estádio do Marcanã stadium. Suppose that all the seats in this stadium are sold out for the first 7 games of the season. How many tickets have been sold for the first 7 games?

Strategy   Use place value.

Step 1   Set up the problem you can use to solve.

$$
\begin{array}{r}
78{,}838 \\
\times \quad 7 \\
\hline
\end{array}
$$

Step 2   Multiply the ones.

$$
\begin{array}{r}
\overset{5}{78{,}838} \\
\times \quad 7 \\
\hline
6
\end{array}
$$

7×8 ones = 56 ones
56 ones = 5 tens 6 ones
Write the ones and the regrouped tens.

Step 3   Multiply the tens.

$$
\begin{array}{r}
\overset{2\,5}{78{,}838} \\
\times \quad 7 \\
\hline
66
\end{array}
$$

7×3 tens = 21 tens
21 tens + 5 tens = 26 tens
26 tens = 2 hundreds 6 tens
Write the tens and the regrouped hundreds.

Step 4   Multiply the hundreds.

$$
\begin{array}{r}
\overset{5\,2\,5}{78{,}838} \\
\times \quad 7 \\
\hline
866
\end{array}
$$

7×8 hundreds = 56 hundreds
56 hundreds + 2 hundreds = 58 hundreds
58 hundreds = 5 thousands 8 hundreds
Write the hundreds and the regrouped thousands.

Step 5   Multiply the thousands.

$$
\begin{array}{r}
65\ 2\ 5 \\
78{,}838 \\
\times\qquad 7 \\
\hline
1{,}866
\end{array}
$$

7×8 thousands = 56 thousands
56 thousands + 5 thousands = 61 thousands
61 thousands = 6 ten thousands 1 thousand
Write the thousand and the regrouped ten thousands.

Step 6   Multiply the ten thousands.

$$
\begin{array}{r}
65\ 2\ 5 \\
78{,}838 \\
\times\qquad 7 \\
\hline
551{,}866
\end{array}
$$

7×7 ten thousands = 49 ten thousands
49 ten thousands + 6 ten thousands = 55 ten thousands
Write the ten thousands.

Solution   For the first 7 games, 551,866 tickets have been sold.

When you multiply by a 2-digit number, you can multiply first by the ones digit, then by the tens digit. This will give you two **partial products**. Then add the two partial products to get the final product.

Example 2

A college football stadium has 24 sections of seats. Each section contains 386 seats. What is the seating capacity of this stadium?

Strategy   Use place value and partial products.

Step 1   Set up the problem you can use to solve.

$$
\begin{array}{r}
386 \\
\times\ 24 \\
\hline
\end{array}
$$

Step 2   Multiply by the ones.

$$
\begin{array}{r}
3\,2 \\
386 \\
\times\ 24 \\
\hline
1544
\end{array}
$$

386×4 ones = 1,544 ones = 1,544
Write the partial product of the ones.

Step 3   Cross out the regrouped numbers. Then multiply by the tens.

$$
\begin{array}{r}
\overset{\scriptstyle 1\ 1}{\cancel{}\cancel{}} \\
386 \\
\times\ 24 \\
\hline
1544 \\
7720 \\
\end{array}
$$

386 × 2 tens = 772 tens = 7,720

Write the partial product of the tens.

Step 4   Add the partial products.

$$
\begin{array}{r}
\overset{\scriptstyle 1\ 1}{\cancel{}\cancel{}} \\
386 \\
\times\ 24 \\
\hline
1544 \\
+\ 7720 \\
\hline
9{,}264 \\
\end{array}
$$

Solution   The seating capacity of the college football stadium is 9,264 people.

Multiplying by a 3-digit number is similar to multiplying by a 2-digit number. The difference is that you will have 3 partial products to add.

Example 3
Multiply 3,218 × 456.

Strategy   Use place value and partial products.

Step 1   Set up the problem. Multiply by the ones.

$$
\begin{array}{r}
\overset{\scriptstyle 1\ 14}{3{,}218} \\
\times\ 456 \\
\hline
19308 \\
\end{array}
$$

3,218 × 6 ones = 19,308 ones = 19,308

Step 2   Multiply by the tens.

$$
\begin{array}{r}
\scriptstyle 1 \quad\; 4 \\[-2pt]
\cancel{1}\;\cancel{14} \\[-2pt]
3{,}218 \\
\times\;\;\; 456 \\
\hline
19308 \\
\mathbf{160900}
\end{array}
$$

$3{,}218 \times 5 \text{ tens} = 16{,}090 \text{ tens} = 160{,}900$

Step 3   Multiply by the hundreds.

$$
\begin{array}{r}
\scriptstyle 3 \\[-2pt]
\cancel{1}\;\;\cancel{4} \\[-2pt]
\cancel{1}\;\cancel{14} \\[-2pt]
3{,}218 \\
\times\;\; 456 \\
\hline
19308 \\
+\,160900 \\
\hline
\mathbf{1287200}
\end{array}
$$

$3{,}218 \times 4 \text{ hundreds} = 12{,}872 \text{ hundreds} = 1{,}287{,}200$

Step 4   Add the three partial products.

$$
\begin{array}{r}
\scriptstyle 3 \\[-2pt]
\cancel{1}\;\;\cancel{4} \\[-2pt]
\cancel{1}\;\cancel{14} \\[-2pt]
3{,}218 \\
\times\;\; 456 \\
\hline
19308 \\
160900 \\
+\,1287200 \\
\hline
\mathbf{1{,}467{,}408}
\end{array}
$$

Solution $3{,}218 \times 456 = 1{,}467{,}408$

Multiply 4,908 × 63.

Set up the problem.

Write the steps for solving this problem.

First, multiply by the _____.

Then, multiply by the _____.

Finally, add the _____ _____.

Show your work.

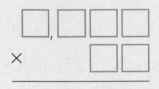

The final product is _____.

4,908 × 63 = _____

1 Raul correctly used place value and partial products to multiply 3,059 by 426. Is each step a step that Raul could have taken in his work? Select Yes or No.

A. Multiply 3,059 by 4. ○ Yes ○ No

B. Multiply 3,059 by 6. ○ Yes ○ No

C. Multiply 3,059 by 2 tens. ○ Yes ○ No

D. Add 18,354; 61,180; and 1,223,600. ○ Yes ○ No

E. Add 18,354; 6,118; and 12,236. ○ Yes ○ No

2 Some college students had a goal of earning $25,000 last year at work. The amount of money each earned is shown. For each amount in the table, indicate with an "X" whether the total earnings met or did not meet the goal.

Total Earnings	Met Goal	Did Not Meet Goal
$478 per week for 52 weeks		
$563 per week for 48 weeks		
$559 per week for 45 weeks		
$602 per week for 37 weeks		

3 Multiply 364 × 257 using partial products. Select True or False for each statement.

A. One partial product is 1,820. ○ True ○ False

B. One partial product is 73,800. ○ True ○ False

C. One partial product is 2,548. ○ True ○ False

D. The total product is 93,548. ○ True ○ False

E. The total product is 78,168. ○ True ○ False

4 Last month, a travel agency in New York City offered tickets for flights to Tokyo, Japan, and to Sydney, Australia. The cost of one round trip ticket to each city is shown on the map.

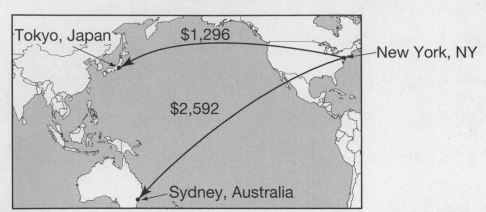

The travel agency sold $54,432 in tickets during this offer. Select tickets the agency could have sold. Circle all that apply.

A. 42 tickets to Tokyo and 0 tickets to Sydney

B. 24 tickets to Tokyo and 9 tickets to Sydney

C. 35 tickets to Tokyo and 4 tickets to Sydney

D. 14 tickets to Tokyo and 14 tickets to Sydney

5 Tamir and Lana found the product of the problem shown below.

725 × 493

- In his work, Tamir multiplied 700 by 400, 20 by 90, and 5 by 3 and then added the partial products.

- In her work, Lana added the partial products 2,175; 65,250; and 290,000 to get her answer.

Which student solved the problem correctly? _____

Describe an error that one of the students made.

6 The city of Rockville is holding a concert to raise money for a new park. Two thousand, four hundred seventy-six adult tickets and 938 student tickets have been sold. How much money has been raised from ticket sales? Show your work.

$ _____

Support Your Local Park

Concert Tickets

Adult	Student
$32	$15

7 Elephants can eat up to 375 pounds of vegetation and drink up to 40 gallons of water each day. How much vegetation could an elephant eat in a year? (Hint: 1 year = 365 days)

_____

Describe the steps you used to solve the problem.

8 Rose and Theo each used place value and partial products to multiply 924 × 576. They compared their work. They both had the right answer, but their work was different. Show two ways this problem can be solved using place value and partial products.

9 In science class, Chloe and her partner checked each other's vital signs: pulse, respiration rate, and temperature. Chloe's vital signs are shown in the table.

Chloe's Vital Signs

Vital Sign	Measurement
Pulse (heart rate)	94 beats per minute
Respiration rate	18 breaths per minute
Temperature	98.7° F

Part A

Chloe said that if her vital signs remained the same throughout one day, she would take about 26,000 breaths in that day. Is Chloe correct? Justify your answer.
(Hints: 1 hour = 60 minutes, 1 day = 24 hours)

Part B

Chloe also said that if her heart rate stays the same throughout the day, her heart would beat about 19,000 times in one day. Is Chloe correct? Justify your answer.

Dividing Whole Numbers

You can use models to help you divide.

Find 187 ÷ 11.

Model the **dividend** 187 as 1 hundred, 8 tens, and 7 ones. The **divisor** is 11. Regroup the hundred and tens. There are 17 groups of 11 in 187. The **quotient** is 17. So, 187 ÷ 11 = 17.

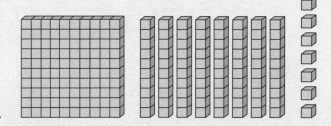

Example 1

Mr. Chen paid $168 for 14 student tickets to the history museum. What is the cost of 1 ticket?

Strategy   Use place value and models to divide.

Step 1   Find $168 ÷ 14. Place the first digit in the quotient.

You cannot divide 1 hundred by 14.
You can divide 16 tens by 14.
The first digit of the quotient is above the tens place.

$$14\overline{)168}$$

1 hundred 6 tens 8 ones

16 tens 8 ones

Step 2   Divide the tens by 14.

$$\begin{array}{r} 1 \\ 14\overline{)168} \\ -\;14 \\ \hline 2 \end{array}$$

      16 tens ÷ 14
      14 × 1 ten
      16 tens − 14 tens

There are 14 groups of 1 ten-dollar bill. There are 2 tens left over.

Step 3   Divide the ones by 14.

$$\begin{array}{r} 12 \\ 14\overline{)168} \\ -\;14\!\downarrow \\ \hline 28 \\ -\;28 \\ \hline 0 \end{array}$$

      Bring down 8 ones.
      28 ones ÷ 14
      14 × 2 ones
      28 ones − 28 ones

Regroup 2 ten-dollar bills as 20 one-dollar bills. There are 28 ones. There are 14 groups of 2 one-dollar bills.

Step 4   Find the quotient.

There are 14 groups of 1 ten-dollar bill and 2 one-dollar bills, or $12.

$168 ÷ 14 = $12

Step 5   Use multiplication to check your answer.

Multiply the quotient by the divisor. $12 \times 14 = 168$
The product matches the dividend. The solution is correct.

Solution   The cost of one ticket is $12.

Example 2

A company ships puzzles in cartons of 18 puzzles each. How many cartons does the company need for 3,672 puzzles?

Strategy   Use place value to divide.

Step 1   Find $3,672 \div 18$. Place the first digit in the quotient.

You cannot divide 3 thousands by 18.
You can divide 36 hundreds by 18.
The first digit of the quotient is above the hundreds place.

$$\begin{array}{r} \square \\ 18\overline{)3,672} \end{array}$$

Step 2   Divide the hundreds by 18.

$$\begin{array}{r} 2 \\ 18\overline{)3,672} \\ -36 \\ \hline 0 \end{array}$$ 36 hundreds $\div$ 18
18 $\times$ 2 hundreds
36 hundreds $-$ 36 hundreds

Step 3   Divide the tens by 18.

$$\begin{array}{r} 20 \\ 18\overline{)3,672} \\ -36\downarrow \\ \hline 7 \\ -0 \\ \hline 7 \end{array}$$ Bring down the tens.
You cannot divide 7 tens by 18. Place 0 in the quotient.
18 $\times$ 0 tens
7 tens $-$ 0 tens

Step 4   Divide the ones by 18.

$$\begin{array}{r} 204 \\ 18\overline{)3,672} \\ -36 \\ \hline 7 \\ -0\downarrow \\ \hline 72 \\ -72 \\ \hline 0 \end{array}$$ Bring down 2 ones.

72 ones $\div$ 18
18 $\times$ 4 ones
72 ones $-$ 72 ones

Solution   The company needs 204 cartons to ship 3,672 puzzles.

Sometimes there will be a **remainder** after you complete the division.

Example 3
Find 1,115 ÷ 3.

Strategy Use place value to divide.

Step 1 Place the first digit in the quotient.

$$3\overline{)1,115}$$ You cannot divide 1 thousand by 3.

$$3\overline{)1,115}$$ You can divide 11 hundreds by 3.

The first digit of the quotient is above the hundreds place.

Step 2 Divide the hundreds by 3.

$$
\begin{array}{r}
3 \\
3\overline{)1,115} \\
-9 \\
\hline
2
\end{array}
$$

11 hundreds ÷ 3
3 × 3 hundreds
11 hundreds − 9 hundreds

Step 3 Divide the tens by 3.

$$
\begin{array}{r}
37 \\
3\overline{)1,115} \\
-9\downarrow \\
\hline
21 \\
-21 \\
\hline
0
\end{array}
$$

Bring down 1 ten.
21 tens ÷ 3
3 × 7 tens
21 tens − 21 tens

Step 4 Divide the ones by 3.

$$
\begin{array}{r}
371 \\
3\overline{)1,115} \\
-9 \\
\hline
21 \\
-21 \\
\hline
5 \\
-3 \\
\hline
2
\end{array}
$$

Bring down 5 ones.

5 ones ÷ 3
3 × 1 ones
5 ones − 3 ones

You cannot divide the remaining 2 ones by 3. The remainder is 2.

Solution 1,115 ÷ 3 = 371 R2

Example 4

There are 2,045 students in a national research project. The project leaders formed teams of 15 students. How many teams did they form?

Strategy   **Use place value to divide.**

Step 1   Find $2{,}045 \div 15$. Place the first digit in the quotient.

You cannot divide 2 thousands by 15.
You can divide 20 hundreds by 15.

The first digit of the quotient is above the hundreds place.

Step 2   Divide the hundreds by 15.

$$
\begin{array}{r}
1 \\
15\overline{)2{,}045} \\
-15 \\
\hline
5
\end{array}
$$

20 hundreds $\div$ 15
15×1 hundreds
20 hundreds $-$ 15 hundreds

Step 3   Divide the tens by 15.

$$
\begin{array}{r}
13 \\
15\overline{)2{,}045} \\
-15\downarrow \\
\hline
54 \\
-45 \\
\hline
9
\end{array}
$$

Bring down the tens.
54 tens $\div$ 15
15×3 tens
54 tens $-$ 45 tens

Step 4   Divide the ones by 15.

$$
\begin{array}{r}
136 \\
15\overline{)2{,}045} \\
-15 \\
\hline
54 \\
-45\downarrow \\
\hline
95 \\
-90 \\
\hline
5
\end{array}
$$

Bring down the ones.

95 ones $\div$ 15
15×6 ones
95 ones $-$ 90 ones

You cannot divide 5 ones by 15. The remainder is 5. This means that there are 5 students left after 136 teams are formed.

$2{,}045 \div 15 = 136 \text{ R}5$

Step 5   Check your answer.

Use multiplication. Add the remainder to the product.

$136 \times 15 = 2,040$

$2,040 + 5 = 2,045$

The answer is correct because 2,045 matches the dividend.

Solution   The leaders formed 136 teams of 15 students each.

2 COACHED EXAMPLE

Find 1,236 ÷ 19.

You cannot divide 1 _____ by 19.

You cannot divide 12 _____ by 19.

You can divide 123 _____ by 19.

The first digit of the quotient is above the _____ place.

$$19\overline{)1,236}$$

Check the answer: _____ × _____ = _____

_____ + _____ = _____

$1,236 \div 19 =$ _____

1 Emily used place-value models to find 182 ÷ 13.

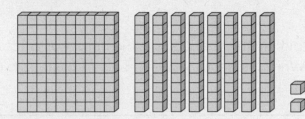

Draw a picture to show how Emily could have used the models to divide.
Then find the quotient. Use a separate piece of paper if necessary.

The quotient is _____.

2 Stefan solved the division problem below.

2,071 ÷ 19

Select True or False for each statement.

A. The first digit in the quotient is in the hundreds place. ○ True ○ False

B. There's a remainder of 17. ○ True ○ False

C. The quotient is 109. ○ True ○ False

D. The solution is 190 R1 ○ True ○ False

3 A company made 1,918 bars of handmade soap. It packed 8 bars of soap in each gift box. Circle the numbers that make the statement true.

238		4
The company packed 239 gift boxes, with 5 bars left over.		
240		6

4 Mandy and Jake worked together on the division problem below.

1,260 ÷ 28

Mandy said the first digit in the quotient is in the hundreds place. Jake said the first digit is in the tens place. Which student is correct? Describe a possible error that one of the students could have made.

5 Use numbers from the box to write the quotient for each division problem.

Division Expression	Quotient
3,155 ÷ 15	
3,314 ÷ 16	
2,484 ÷ 12	
2,310 ÷ 11	

207

207 R2

210

210 R5

6 Is the quotient for the division problem 43 R5? Select Yes or No.

A. 607 ÷ 14   ○ Yes   ○ No

B. 735 ÷ 17   ○ Yes   ○ No

C. 994 ÷ 23   ○ Yes   ○ No

D. 1,548 ÷ 36   ○ Yes   ○ No

E. 1,726 ÷ 40   ○ Yes   ○ No

F. 2,241 ÷ 52   ○ Yes   ○ No

7 Schools, classrooms, and students received equal numbers of flyers about the state fair. Which solution is true? Circle all that apply.

   A. 18 classrooms received 5,850 flyers. Each classroom received 325 flyers.

   B. 6 schools received 8,160 flyers. Each school received 136 flyers.

   C. 23 students shared 416 flyers. Each student received 18 flyers.
       2 flyers were left over.

   D. 3 schools received 1,774 flyers. Each school received 591 flyers.
       3 flyers were left over.

   E. A teacher handed out 532 flyers to 19 students. Each student received 28 flyers.

8 Find the quotient to each division problem. Write the problem in the correct box.

| $1,445 \div 17$ | $1,500 \div 20$ | $1,050 \div 14$ | $1,350 \div 18$ |

75	85

9 A kite company made 2,872 kites for a kite festival. It made an equal number of 8 different types of kites.

Part A

How many of each type did the shop make? _____

Part B

The company received kite orders from 13 different stores. It sent the same number of kites to each store. What is the most number of kites the company could have sent to each store? Explain your reasoning.

10 Ricardo says that he needs 308 plastic sleeves for his comic book collection. He has 1,234 comics. Each sleeve holds 4 comics. Do you agree? Use words, numbers, or a model to explain your reasoning.

```




```

11 Pria used either blue, gold, or red sequins to make costumes.

- blue sequins: 18 per costume

- gold sequins: 22 per costume

- red sequins: 16 per costume

The table shows the total number of sequins Pria had of each color.

Color	Number of Sequins
Blue	2,142
Gold	1,896
Red	3,208

Write the greatest number of costumes Pria could have made for each color of sequins.

Costumes with blue sequins _____

Costumes with gold sequins _____

Costumes with red sequins _____

Explain how you chose the number of costumes with red sequins.

```




```

LESSON **11**

5.NBT.7

Adding and Subtracting Decimals

1 GETTING THE IDEA

You can use place-value models to add and subtract decimals.

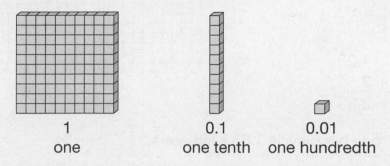

1
one

0.1
one tenth

0.01
one hundredth

You can combine ones, tenths, and hundredths to show addition. You can remove hundredths, tenths, and ones from a model to show subtraction.

Example 1

Elsa rode her bicycle 1.28 kilometers to the park. She rode 2.55 kilometers around the park. How many kilometers did Elsa ride her bicycle?

Strategy   Use models to add.

Step 1   Write a problem you can use to solve.

You want to know how many kilometers Elsa rode in all.
Add to find the total.

$1.28 + 2.55$

Step 2   Add the hundredths.

$8 + 5 = 13$ hundredths

Regroup 13 hundredths as 1 tenth 3 hundredths.

$$
\begin{array}{r}
\overset{1}{1}.28 \\
+\ 2.55 \\
\hline
3
\end{array}
$$

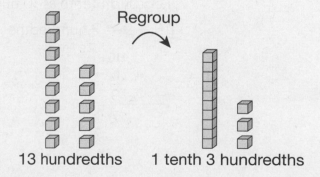

Regroup

13 hundredths   1 tenth 3 hundredths

Step 3	Add the tenths. Remember to add the regrouped tenth.

$1 + 2 + 5 = 8$ tenths

Write the decimal point in the sum.

$$
\begin{array}{r}
\overset{1}{1.28} \\
+\ 2.55 \\
\hline
.83
\end{array}
$$

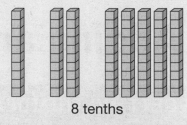

8 tenths

Step 4	Add the ones.

$1 + 2 = 3$ ones

$$
\begin{array}{r}
\overset{1}{1.28} \\
+\ 2.55 \\
\hline
3.83
\end{array}
$$

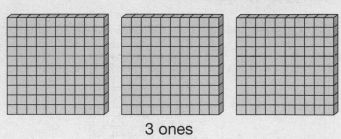

3 ones

Solution   Elsa rode her bicycle 3.83 kilometers.

Example 2

Emilio bought cheddar cheese and Swiss cheese to make grilled cheese sandwiches. The cheddar weighed 4.56 pounds. The Swiss weighed 2.79 pounds. How many more pounds did the cheddar cheese weigh than the Swiss cheese?

Strategy   Use models to subtract.

Step 1	Write a problem you can use to solve.

You want to know how many more pounds the cheddar cheese weighed than the Swiss cheese. Subtract to find how much more.

$4.56 - 2.79$

Step 2	Subtract the hundredths.

There are not enough hundredths to subtract 9. Regroup 1 tenth as 10 hundredths.

$16 - 9 = 7$ hundredths

$$
\begin{array}{r}
4.5\overset{4\ 16}{6} \\
-\ 2.79 \\
\hline
7
\end{array}
$$

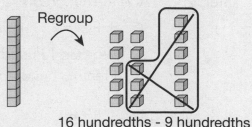

Regroup

16 hundredths - 9 hundredths

Step 3 Subtract the tenths.

There are not enough tenths to subtract 7 tenths.
Regroup 1 whole as 10 tenths.

14 − 7 = 7 tenths

Write the decimal point in the sum.

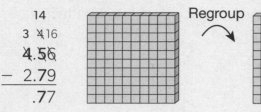

$$\begin{array}{r} {\scriptstyle 14} \\ {\scriptstyle 3\ \cancel{4}\,16} \\ 4.5\cancel{6} \\ -\ 2.79 \\ \hline .77 \end{array}$$

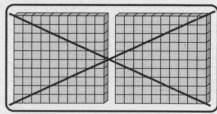

1   14 tenths - 7 tenths

Step 4 Subtract the ones.

3 − 2 = 1 one

$$\begin{array}{r} {\scriptstyle 14} \\ {\scriptstyle 3\ \cancel{4}\,1\cancel{6}} \\ 4.5\cancel{6} \\ -\ 2.79 \\ \hline 1.77 \end{array}$$

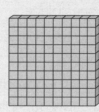

3 ones - 2 ones

Step 5 Check the answer using addition.

Add the difference to 2.79. The sum should be 4.56.

$$\begin{array}{r} {\scriptstyle 1\ 1} \\ 1.77 \\ +\ 2.79 \\ \hline 4.56 \end{array}$$

The sum is 4.56. The answer is correct.

Solution **The cheddar cheese weighed 1.77 pounds more than the Swiss cheese.**

Example 3

Subtract 40 − 15.47.

Strategy   Use place value to subtract.

Step 1   Write the problem in vertical form.

Write 40 as an equivalent decimal in hundredths.

40 = 40.00

Align the decimal points.

$$
\begin{array}{r}
40.00 \\
-\,15.47 \\
\end{array}
$$

Step 2   Subtract the hundredths.

You cannot subtract 7 hundredths from 0 hundredths.

Regroup 1 ten as 10 ones. Record 3 in the tens place.
Record 10 in the ones place.

Regroup 1 one as 10 tenths. Record 9 in the ones place.
Record 10 in the tenths place.

Regroup 1 tenth as 10 hundredths. Record 9 in the tenths place.
Record 10 in the hundredths place.

10 − 7 = 3 hundredths

$$
\begin{array}{r}
{\scriptstyle 9\ \ 9} \\
{\scriptstyle 3\,\backslash\!10\,\backslash\!10\,10} \\
\cancel{40.00} \\
-\,15.47 \\
\hline
.\ \ \ 3 \\
\end{array}
$$

Step 3   Subtract the tenths.

9 − 4 = 5 tenths

$$
\begin{array}{r}
{\scriptstyle 9\ \ 9} \\
{\scriptstyle 3\,\backslash\!10\,\backslash\!10\,10} \\
\cancel{40.00} \\
-\,15.47 \\
\hline
.53 \\
\end{array}
$$

Step 4   Subtract the ones.

$$9 - 5 = 4 \text{ ones}$$

```
    9  9
  3 10 10 10
  40.00
- 15.47
   4.53
```

Step 5   Subtract the tens.

$$3 - 1 = 2 \text{ tens}$$

```
    9  9
  3 10 10 10
  40.00
- 15.47
  24.53
```

Step 6   Check the answer using addition.

```
  1 1 1
  24.53
+ 15.47
  40.00
```

The sum is 40.00. The answer is correct.

Solution $40 - 15.47 = 24.53$

Maya bought a scarf and hat from two different stores. The scarf cost $32.18. The hat cost $19.86. How much did Maya pay in all for the scarf and hat?

Write a problem you can use to solve.

_____ + _____ = ☐

Write the problem in vertical form.

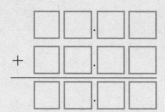

First, I add the _____.

_____ + _____ = _____

Regroup _____ as _____.

Second, I add the _____.

_____ + _____ + _____ = _____

Regroup _____ as _____.

Third, I add the _____.

_____ + _____ + _____ = _____

Regroup _____ as _____.

Fourth, I add the _____.

_____ + _____ + _____ = _____

Write _____ in the sum.

I can use _____ to check the answer.

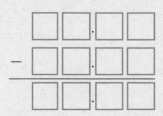

Maya paid _____ in all for the scarf and hat.

1 Add 1.27 + 2.94. You can use the models to help you.

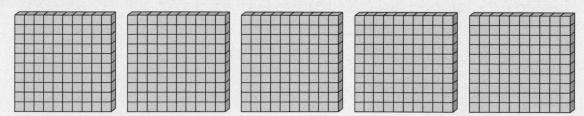

The sum is _____.

2 Draw a line from each problem to its sum or difference.

A. 12.9 + 1.53 •   • 11.46

B. 14.76 − 3.3 •   • 13.62

C. 11.24 + 6.82 •   • 14.43

D. 19.42 − 5.8 •   • 18.06

3 Nami is wrapping packages with green and pink ribbon. She has 11.85 meters of green ribbon and 13.4 meters of pink ribbon.

Part A

How many meters of ribbon does Nami have in all? Show your work.

Part B

How many more meters of pink ribbon are there than green ribbon? Use words, numbers, or a model to justify your answer.

_____ more meters of pink ribbon

4 Lucia used place-value models to find 1.87 + 1.36. Use words or numbers and a drawing to explain how Lucia could have found the sum.

[ ]

The sum is _____.

5 James recorded the miles he walked each month in a spreadsheet.

Which statements are correct? Circle all that apply.

A. James walked 29.53 miles in January and February.

B. James walked 0.44 mile farther in March than in April.

C. James walked 26.33 miles in January and April.

D. James walked 24.4 miles in February and April.

E. James walked 4.69 miles farther in January than in March.

F. James walked 3.4 miles farther in February than in March.

	A	B
1	**Month**	**Miles**
2	January	15.73
3	February	14.8
4	March	11.04
5	April	10.6

6 Use problems from the box to write the addition or subtraction problem for each sum or difference.

Sum or Difference	Problem
4.85	
5.48	
6.23	
7.13	

3.78 + 1.7
5.2 + 1.93
9.8 − 3.57
7.25 − 2.4

7 A cashier received $20 for each item.

Item	Cost
Binder	$12.76
Box of Pencils	$8.24
Markers	$11.53
Padded Envelopes	$15.97

Did the cashier give back the correct change? Select Yes or No.

A. Change for a box of pencils: $11.86　　　○ Yes　○ No

B. Change for binder: $7.24　　　○ Yes　○ No

C. Change for padded envelopes: $4.03　　　○ Yes　○ No

D. Change for markers: $9.57　　　○ Yes　○ No

8 The amount of sleep some animals get each day is shown in the table.

Animal	Sleep Time (hours)
Chimpanzee	9.7
Cow	3.9
Opossum	18
Rabbit	11.4

Select True or False for each statement.

A. Chimpanzees sleep 8.3 fewer hours than opossums.　　　○ True　○ False

B. Rabbits sleep 8.5 hours more than cows.　　　○ True　○ False

C. Cows sleep 5.8 fewer hours than chimpanzees.　　　○ True　○ False

D. Opossums sleep 7.4 hours more than rabbits.　　　○ True　○ False

9 One runner in the table has a time that is 0.2 second faster than another runner.

100-Meter Dash

Runner	Time (seconds)
Jacques Fain	9.13
Lilah Jackson	9.05
Dembe Usa	8.93

Who are the two runners? _____

Who is the faster runner? _____

10 The time it takes some planets to orbit the Sun in Earth years is shown below.

Time to Orbit the Sun in Earth Years

Planet	Mercury	Venus	Mars	Saturn
Time to Orbit Sun	0.24 year	0.62 year	1.88 years	29.46 years

Circle the words and numbers that make the statement true.

27.58		Mercury
Saturn takes 28.24 more Earth years to orbit the Sun than		Venus .
29.84		Mars

11 Hana is rollerblading along an 8-mile trail in Forest Park. She stopped for water after rollerblading 2.4 miles. After another 3.1 miles, she stopped for lunch. How much farther does she have to go to reach the end of the trail? Describe the steps you took to solve the problem.

Multiplying Decimals

1 GETTING THE IDEA

An **area model** is a rectangular model that shows a value in square units. You can use an area model to help you multiply decimals. Use the models below to show the value of the decimals.

One whole = 1   One tenth = 0.1   One hundredth = 0.01

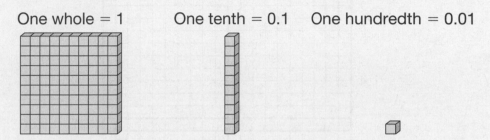

To model any multiplication problem, you can draw a rectangle. Make the length and width of the two factors. The area of the rectangle shows the product.

Here is an area model that can be used to find the product of 2.5 × 1.3.
2.5 is the same as 2 wholes, 5 tenths. Notice that the length of the model is 2.5 units.
1.3 is the same as 1 whole and 3 tenths. Notice that the width of the model is 1.3 units.
The rest of the rectangle is filled with hundredths units.

2.5

1.3

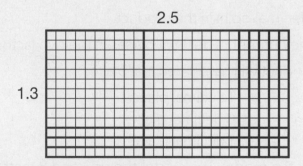

Count the decimal models to find the product.
There are 2 wholes, 11 tenths, and 15 hundredths.
To simplify the product, regroup.

So 2 wholes, 11 tenths, and 15 hundredths = 3 wholes, 2 tenths, and 5 hundredths
1.3 × 2.5 = 3.25

Example 1

Multiply 2 × 1.4.

Strategy   Draw an area model to show the product. Then use place value to multiply.

Step 1   Draw an area model.

Make the model with a length of 2 wholes and the width of 1 whole and 4 tenths.

This completes the rectangle.

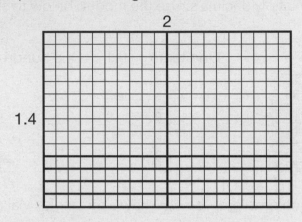

Step 2   Use place value to multiply.

First, multiply as you would with whole numbers.

$$\begin{array}{r} 1.4 \\ \times\ 2 \\ \hline 28 \end{array}$$

Step 3   Place the decimal point in the product.

Add the number of decimal places in the two factors.

The product will have 1 decimal place.

$$\begin{array}{r} 1.4 \\ \times\ 2 \\ \hline 2.8 \end{array}$$
← 1 decimal place
← 0 decimal places
← 1 decimal place

Look at the model. The model shows 2 and 8 tenths, so the product is 2.8.

Solution   1.4 × 2 = 2.8

Example 2

Margo walked 1.2 times around a trail at her local park. The trail is 1.3 miles long. How far did Margo walk?

Strategy   **Use an area model and place value to find the product.**

Step 1   Write a problem you can use to solve.

To find the total distance Margo walked, use multiplication.

1.2×1.3

Step 2   Draw an area model.

Make the model with a length of 1 whole and 3 tenths and the width of 1 whole and 2 tenths.

Fill in the model with hundredths to make a complete rectangle.

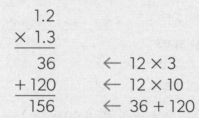

Step 3   Use place value to multiply.

Multiply as you would with whole numbers.

$$
\begin{array}{r}
1.2 \\
\times\ 1.3 \\
\hline
36 \\
+\ 120 \\
\hline
156
\end{array}
$$

$\leftarrow 12 \times 3$
$\leftarrow 12 \times 10$
$\leftarrow 36 + 120$

Step 4   Place the decimal point in the product.

$$
\begin{array}{r}
1.2 \\
\times\ 1.3 \\
\hline
36 \\
+\ 120 \\
\hline
1.56
\end{array}
$$

$\leftarrow$ one decimal place
$\leftarrow$ one decimal place

$\leftarrow$ two decimal places

Look at the model. The model shows 1 whole, 5 tenths, and 6 hundredths.

Solution   **Margo walked 1.56 miles.**

Example 3

Kayla feeds her dog 1.75 cups of food each day. How many cups of food does Kayla feed her dog each week?

Strategy   Use place value.

Step 1   Write a problem you can use to solve.

One week is 7 days. Multiply the number of cups of food by 7.

1.75×7

Step 2   Use place value to multiply.

Multiply as you would with whole numbers.

$$
\begin{array}{r}
{\scriptstyle 5\,3} \\
1.75 \\
\times\ \ \ 7 \\
\hline
1225
\end{array}
$$

Step 3   Place the decimal point in the product.

Add the number of decimal places in the two factors.

The product will have 2 decimal places.

$$
\begin{array}{r}
1.75 \\
\times\ \ \ 7 \\
\hline
12.25
\end{array}
$$
  ← two decimal places
  ← zero decimal places
  ← two decimal places

Step 4   Use estimation to check the reasonableness of your answer.

1.75 cups is about 2 cups.

7×2 cups $= 14$ cups

The product of 12.25 cups is close to 14 cups. The product is reasonable.

Solution   **Kayla feeds her dog 12.25 cups of food each week.**

Example 4

Janette earns $8.25 per hour babysitting. She babysat her neighbor's daughter for 4.5 hours. How much did Janette earn?

Strategy   Use place value.

Step 1   Write a problem you can use to solve.

Multiply the amount Janette earns per hour by the number of hours she babysits.

8.25×4.5

Step 2   Use place value to multiply.

Multiply as you would with whole numbers.

$$
\begin{array}{r}
\overset{1\ 2}{\underset{1\ 2}{}} \\
8.25 \\
\times\ 4.5 \\
\hline
4125 \\
+\ 33000 \\
\hline
37125
\end{array}
$$

Step 3   Place the decimal point in the product.

Add the number of decimal places in the two factors.

The product will have 3 decimal places.

$$
\begin{array}{rl}
8.25 & \leftarrow \text{ two decimal places} \\
\times\ 4.5 & \leftarrow \text{ one decimal place} \\
\hline
37.125 & \leftarrow \text{ three decimal places}
\end{array}
$$

Step 4   Compare your answer to the question asked.

Money can have only two decimal places, so the answer must be rounded to the nearest hundredth.

$37.125 rounds to $37.13.

Step 5   Use estimation to check the reasonableness of your answer.

$8.25 is about $8.

4.5 is about 5.

$8 \times 5 = 40$

Because $37.13 is close to $40, the answer is reasonable.

Solution   **Janette earned $37.13 babysitting.**

Multiply 4.71 × 0.2.

First, multiply as you would with whole numbers.

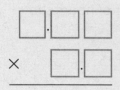

4.71 has ___2___ decimal place(s).

0.2 has ___1___ decimal place(s).

So, the product will have ___3___ decimal place(s).

4.71 × 0.2 = ___.942___

1 Write an equation that is represented by the area model.

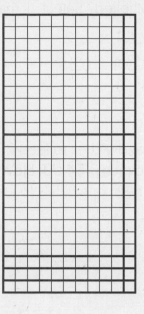

_____ × _____ = _____

2 Circle the number that makes the equation true.

$$6.1 \times \boxed{\begin{array}{c} 416 \\ 41.6 \\ \bcancel{4.16} \\ 0.416 \end{array}} = 25.376$$

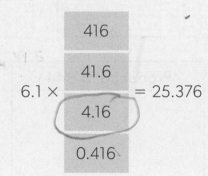

3 Derrick needs to find the area of a large poster. The poster measures 1.3 meters by 1.1 meters. Use an area model, words, or numbers to justify your answer.

$$\begin{array}{r} 1.3 \\ \times \; 1.1 \quad 1.4.3 \\ \hline 1.43 \end{array}$$

The area of the poster is __1.43__ square meters.

4 Yoshi multiplied two numbers. Her product contained 3 decimal places. Which pair of numbers could Yoshi have multiplied? Select all that apply.

A. 3.12 × 4.1   D. 5.1 × 3.12

B. 4.1 × 6.2   E. 0.9 × 0.55

C. 8.33 × 9

5 Ms. Nichols bought enough sandwiches to feed 28 people. Each sandwich serves 2 people. The cost of one sandwich is $4.99. How much did Ms. Nichols pay for the sandwiches? Use words, numbers, or models to justify your answer.

> 4.99
> 2
>
> 18
> +180
> 800
> 990

6 Find each product. Write the problem in the correct box.

| 1.87 × 3 | 3.1 × 1.24 | 41.2 × 0.2 | 2.06 × 4 | 0.62 × 6.2 |

Product of 8.24	Product of 3.844	Product of 5.61

7 Justine correctly multiplied the decimals shown. How can the product be correct without three decimal places?

8.5 × 2.34 = 19.89

8 The multiplication problem below is incorrect.

$$
\begin{array}{r}
4.21 \\
\times\ 8.3 \\
\hline
1263 \\
+\ 3368 \\
\hline
4.631
\end{array}
$$

Part A

Explain the error in the problem.

Part B

Find the correct product.

9 Marvin wrote the following clues to describe a multiplication sentence.

• The product is close in value to 10.

• Both factors are decimal numbers.

• The product has three decimal places.

• One factor is greater than 1. The other factor is less than 1.

Write a multiplication equation that fits these clues. Explain how you created your answer.

10 Luka is eating crackers. Each serving has 1.6 grams of fat. She ate 0.75 serving of crackers at lunch. She is now eating 1.5 servings of crackers as a snack. How many grams of fat did Luka eat all together? Explain how you solved the problem.

11 Jin needs 0.8 gram of carbon for an experiment. She needs 4.15 times as much water. Jin says that she needs less than 4.15 grams of water.

Part A

Is Jin correct? Explain your reasoning.

Part B

How much water does Jin need for the experiment? Show your work.

LESSON 13

Dividing Decimals

5.NBT.7

1 GETTING THE IDEA

You can use decimal models to show decimal division.

Divide 3.6 ÷ 3. Start by modeling 3.6.

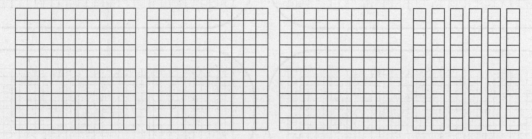

Break the whole number part into 3 equal groups. Each group will have 1 whole.

Then break the 6 tenths into 3 equal groups. Each group will have 2 tenths.

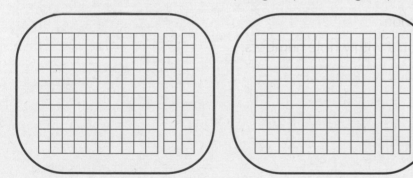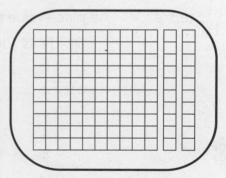

Each group contains 1 whole and 2 tenths or 1.2.

So, 3.6 ÷ 3 = 1.2.

Lesson 13: Dividing Decimals **113**

Example 1

Divide 12.4 ÷ 4.

Strategy   Make a model to find the quotient. Then use place value to divide.

Step 1   Show 12.4. Divide the models into 4 equal groups.

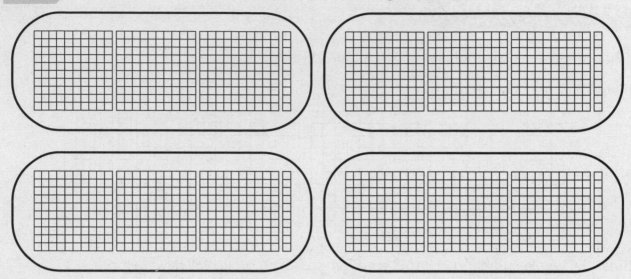

Each group contains 3 wholes and 1 tenth.

Step 2   Use place value to divide.

Divide as you would with whole numbers.

$$
\begin{array}{r}
3\ 1 \\
4\overline{)12.4} \\
-12\!\downarrow \\
\hline
0\ 4 \\
-4 \\
\hline
0
\end{array}
$$

Step 3   Place the decimal point in the quotient.

The decimal point in the quotient is directly above the decimal point in the dividend.

$$
\begin{array}{r}
3.1 \\
\uparrow \\
4\overline{)12.4}
\end{array}
$$

The model shows the quotient is 3.1.

Solution   12.4 ÷ 4 = 3.1

Example 2

Genevieve bought 9 bottles of apple juice for the school picnic. She spent a total of $16.56 on apple juice. Each bottle of juice cost the same. What was the price for one bottle of juice?

Strategy   Use place value to divide.

Step 1   Write a problem you can use to solve.

Divide the total amount Genevieve spent by the number of bottles of juice she bought.

$16.56 \div 9$

Step 2   Use place value. Divide as you would with whole numbers.

$$
\begin{array}{r}
1\,84 \\
9)\overline{16.56} \\
-9\downarrow \\
\hline
7\,5 \\
-7\,2\downarrow \\
\hline
3\,6 \\
-3\,6 \\
\hline
0
\end{array}
$$

Step 3   Place the decimal point directly above the decimal point in the dividend.

$$
\begin{array}{r}
1.84 \\
9)\overline{16.56}
\end{array}
$$

You can use estimation to check that the decimal point is in the right place.

16.56 is about 17.

17 divided by 9 is more than 1 but not quite 2.

So it makes sense that the quotient is 1.84 not 18.4.

Step 4   Use multiplication to check your answer.

Multiply the quotient by the divisor.

$$
\begin{array}{r}
{}^{7\ 3} \\
1.84 \\
\times \quad 9 \\
\hline
16.56
\end{array}
$$

The product is the same as the dividend. The answer is correct.

Solution   Genevieve spent $1.84 on each bottle of apple juice.

Example 3

Mrs. Jarvis works at the school cafeteria. She has 87.5 ounces of ground beef. She is making meatballs that each weigh 2.5 ounces. How many meatballs can Mrs. Jarvis make?

Strategy Use place value. Change the divisor to a whole number.

Step 1 Write a problem you can use to solve.

Divide the number of ounces of ground beef by the number of ounces per meatball.

$87.5 \div 2.5$

Step 2 Change the divisor to a whole number.

Multiply the divisor by 10. Multiply the dividend by the same value.

$$87.5 \quad \div \quad 2.5$$
$$\downarrow \times 10 \downarrow \quad \times 10$$
$$875 \quad \div \quad 25$$

$2.5\overline{)87.5}$ becomes $25\overline{)875}$

Multiplying by 10 moves the decimal point one place to the right. This makes the divisor a whole number.

Step 3 Divide the new numbers.

$$
\begin{array}{r}
35 \\
25\overline{)875} \\
-75\downarrow \\
\hline
125 \\
-125 \\
\hline
0
\end{array}
$$

$87.5 \div 2.5 = 35$

Step 4 Use multiplication to check your answer.

Multiply the quotient by the divisor.

$$
\begin{array}{r}
\overset{1}{}\overset{2}{} \\
35 \\
\times\ 2.5 \\
\hline
175 \\
+\ 700 \\
\hline
87.5
\end{array}
$$

The product is the same as the dividend. The answer is correct.

Solution Mrs. Jarvis can make 35 meatballs.

Example 4

Divide 38.58 ÷ 0.12.

Strategy   Use place value. Change the divisor to a whole number.

Step 1   Change the divisor to a whole number.

Multiply the divisor by 100. Multiply the dividend by the same value.

$$38.58 \div 0.12$$

$$\downarrow \times 100 \quad \downarrow \times 100$$

$$3{,}858 \div 12$$

0.12)38.58 becomes 12)3858

Step 2   Divide the new numbers.

```
        321
   12)3858
     - 36↓|
        25|
      - 24↓
         18
       - 12
          6
```

Step 3   Continue to divide until there is no remainder.

Write a decimal point and zero to the right of the dividend.

Write the decimal point in the quotient and continue to divide.

Remember, 3,858 is the same as 3,858.0.

```
        321.5
   12)3858.0
     - 36↓|
        25|
      - 24↓
         18
       - 12↓
         60
       - 60
          0
```

$$38.58 \div 0.12 = 321.5$$

| Step 4 | Use multiplication to check your answer. |

Multiply the quotient by 0.12.

$$\begin{array}{r} 1 \\ 321.5 \\ \times\ \ 0.12 \\ \hline 6430 \\ +\ 32150 \\ \hline 38.580 \end{array}$$

Since 38.580 is the same as 38.58, the product is the same as the dividend. The answer is correct.

Solution $38.58 \div 0.12 = 321.5$

② COACHED EXAMPLE

Divide $71.4 \div 2.8$.

Change the divisor to a whole number.

Multiply the divisor by _____. Multiply the dividend by the same number.

71.4 becomes _____.

2.8 becomes _____.

Divide the new numbers. Divide until there is no remainder. Write a decimal point and a _____ to the right of the dividend to complete the division.

$$\overline{)}$$

Use multiplication to check your answer.

Multiply _____ and _____.

The product matches the _____, so the answer is correct.

$71.4 \div 2.8 =$ _____

1 Draw a line to match each division equation to the multiplication equation that could be used to check the quotient.

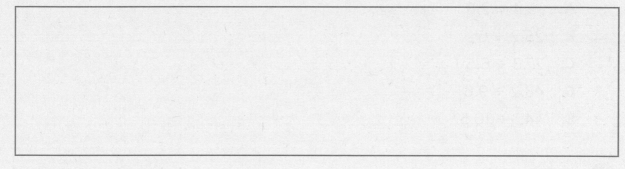

A. $28.84 \div 7.21 = 4$ •   • $4 \times 72.1 = 288.4$

B. $2.884 \div 4 = 0.721$ •   • $4 \times 0.721 = 2.884$

C. $288.4 \div 72.1 = 4$ •   • $4 \times 7.21 = 28.84$

2 Ushma downloaded 8 songs. The total cost of the songs was $15.92. Each song cost the same amount. What was the price for one song? Justify your answer using words, numbers, or a model.

Each song cost $_____.

3 Marta and Jake worked together on the division problem below.

$45.21 \div 8.22$

- Marta said the dividend and divisor should be multiplied by 10 to make each number a whole number.

- Jake said that the dividend and divisor should be multiplied by 100 to make each number a whole number.

With which student do you agree? Explain your answer.

4 Gina saves quarters. She has $17.75 in quarters. How many quarters does she have? Show your solution in two ways. Use division to show one way. Use words, numbers, or models for the second way.

5 Which division problem has a quotient of 4.2? Circle all that apply.

A. $15.4 \div 2.8$

B. $25.2 \div 6$

C. $27.3 \div 6.5$

D. $43.2 \div 9.6$

E. $44.1 \div 10.5$

6 Look at the two division problems below. Will they have the same quotient? Use words, pictures, or numbers to help explain your answer.

$7.4\overline{)92.5}$ $\qquad$ $74\overline{)925}$

7 Juliette and her two brothers spent $45.75 on flowers for their grandmother.

Part A

Each person will chip in the same amount. How much will each person pay?
Show your work.

Each person will pay _____.

Part B

Juliette's mom decided to chip in $15. Now how much will Juliette and her brothers each pay if they share the amount remaining?

Each person will pay _____.

8 Ester packed 9 boxes inside of a crate. Each box weighed the same amount. If the crate weighed a total of 92.16 kilograms, how much did each box weigh?

_____ kilograms

9 Lilah completed the division problem below.

$$7.84 \div 2$$

Select True or False for each statement.

A. The first step of the division is to multiply 7.84 and 2 by 10. ○ True ○ False

B. The quotient will be a whole number. ○ True ○ False

C. The quotient multiplied by 2 will equal 7.84. ○ True ○ False

D. The first digit of the quotient will be in the ones place. ○ True ○ False

E. The quotient will have two decimal places. ○ True ○ False

10 Nathaniel measured the height of one shelf on his bookcase. He wants to know which books will fit on the shelf. The shelf is 22.86 centimeters tall. He measured it again with an inch ruler. The shelf is 9 inches tall.

Part A

Write an equation you could use to find the number of centimeters in 1 inch.

_____

Part B

Solve the equation you wrote in Part A. Show your work.

Part C

The top shelf of Nathaniel's bookcase is 12 inches tall. How many centimeters tall is the top shelf?

_____

DOMAIN 2 REVIEW

1 The cost of a ticket at a concert hall depends on where the seat is located. The section number, cost per ticket, and number of seats in each section are given in the table below.

Section Number	Cost per Ticket	Number of Seats
1	$127	72
2	$145	58
3	$158	86
4	$191	38

A charity organization buys all of the tickets for Sections 1 and 2 for an event. How much will the charity organization pay for the tickets? Show your work.

The charity organization will pay _____ for the tickets.

2 The lengths of different species of sea turtles are shown in the table.

Turtle Species	Length (in meters)
Flatback	0.9
Green	1.2
Kemp's Ridley	0.6
Leatherback	2.4

Select True or False for each statement.

A. Green turtles are 0.6 meter longer than Kemp's Ridley turtles. ○ True ○ False

B. Leatherback turtles are 0.05 meter longer than Flatback turtles. ○ True ○ False

C. Green turtles are 1.2 meters shorter than Leatherback turtles. ○ True ○ False

D. Kemp's Ridley turtles are 2.2 meters shorter than Leatherback turtles. ○ True ○ False

3 Circle the number that makes each sentence true.

217.48			217.41
217.5	< 217.46	217.46 >	217.46
217.046			217.552

4 Felipe is giving a speech at graduation. The first part of his speech is 2.35 minutes long. The second part of his speech is 2.41 minutes long. Felipe's entire speech can take no longer than 5 minutes. Is Felipe's speech less than 5 minutes? Use words, numbers, or a model to justify your answer.

5 Find the first digit of the quotient. Is the first digit in the tens or hundreds place? Write the division expression in the correct box.

1,615 ÷ 17	2,332 ÷ 12	1,450 ÷ 14	1,350 ÷ 19

Tens	Hundreds

6 Alejandro rounded the number 76.518 to 76.5. Jiro rounded the same number to 76.52. Who is correct? Explain your reasoning.

---

7 Choose a digit from the box to complete the second factor so that the product will have 2 decimal places.

$$7.2 \times 4.6 \text{\_\_\_\_\_}$$

1
3
5
9

8 Mrs. Blanda's truck holds 19.7 gallons of gas. She used 4 full tanks of gas last month and paid $3 for each gallon. How much did Mrs. Blanda spend on gas last month? Show your work.

---

9 Use numbers from the box to complete the comparison statements about the digits in 288.99.

The digit in the ones place is $\frac{1}{10}$ of _____.

The digit in the hundredths place is $\frac{1}{10}$ of _____.

The digit in the tens place is 10 times as much as _____.

The digit in the tenths place is 10 times as much as _____.

80
8
0.9
0.09

10 Caleb is sorting 1,368 food cans into boxes. He sorts 12 cans into each box. How many boxes will Caleb need? Use words, numbers, or a model to explain your reasoning.

11 Paula correctly compared the numbers 317.452 and 317.401. Which statement could she have made when describing her reasoning? Circle all that apply.

 A. Since 4 tenths = 4 tenths, I need to move to the next place value to compare.

 B. The digits in the hundreds place are different.

 C. The values of the digits in the hundredths place will tell me which number is greater.

 D. Since 5 hundredths > 0 hundredths, 317.452 > 317.401.

 E. Since 7 ones = 7 ones, 317.452 = 317.401.

12 At the 2012 Olympics, the team that won the gold medal for the women's 4 × 100 relay had a time of forty and eighty-two hundredths seconds. The time for the team that won the silver medal can be found using the clues below.

 • The tens digit is the same as the tens digit in the gold medal time.

 • The ones digit is greater than the gold medal time by 1.

 • The tens digit is 100 times greater than the tenths digit.

 • The hundredths digit is the same as the ones digit.

 The team that won the silver medal had a time of _____ seconds.

13 In the division problem 64.94 ÷ 8.5, should the dividend and divisor be multiplied by 10 or 100 to make the divisor a whole number? Explain your answer.

14 Select True or False for each equation.

A. $2.1 \times 10^1 = 2.1 \div 10$ ○ True   ○ False

B. $2.1 \div 10^1 > 0.21 \times 10^2$ ○ True   ○ False

C. $210 \div 10^2 > 2.1 \div 10^1$ ○ True   ○ False

D. $210 \div 10^3 = 0.021 \times 10^1$ ○ True   ○ False

15 Ayako is completing a sewing project with 2 classmates. Each group will create small squares for a quilt to donate to a hospital. His group is given 16.8 square yards of fabric.

Part A

Each member of the group will work with the same amount of fabric. How many square yards will each member receive? Show your work.

Part B

There are 12 different groups of students in Ayako's class. Each group received the same amount of fabric as Ayako's group. How much fabric did his class use in all? Show your work.

Making Trail Mix

You are making trail mix to share with your class.

- There are 10 people in your class. Each person will get a bag of trail mix.
- You would like to give at least 1 cup of trail mix to each person, but each bag can hold no more than 1.5 cups.
- You would like for each person to get the same amount of trail mix.

Part A The recipe calls for the ingredients shown at right. Find how many cups of mix the recipe makes by finding the total amount of the ingredients. Show your work.

Part B You would like to put at least 1 cup of trail mix in each person's bag. Determine how many times you will increase the recipe so that each person will get one bag of trail mix. Explain your decision. Include the amount of trail mix you will put in each bag.

Trail Mix

Ingredients
2.5 cups toasted corn cereal
1 cup oats
0.5 cup chopped walnuts
1 cup chopped dried apricots

Part C Rewrite the ingredients list to show how much of each you will need when you increase the recipe.

Part D The table below gives information about the package size and cost of the ingredients at one store.

Ingredient	Package Size	Cost of Package	Packages Needed	Cost
Corn cereal	12 cups	$3.39		
Oats	5 cups	$3.99		
Chopped walnuts	0.75 cup	$1.99		
Dried apricots	1.45 cups	$2.18		

Complete the last two columns to find the cost of each ingredient needed to make the trail mix. Then find the total cost of making the trail mix. Show your work.

Part E How much of each ingredient will you have left over? Show your work.

Part F Review the amount of trail mix you plan to make and put in each bag, the total cost of your plan, and the leftover ingredients. Do you want to change the amount of mix you will put in each bag? Explain your decision.

DOMAIN 3

Number and Operations – Fractions

Adding and Subtracting Fractions and Mixed Numbers

A **mixed number** is a number that has a whole-number part and a fraction part.

whole number

↓

$15\frac{2}{5}$

↑

fraction

To add and subtract fractions and mixed numbers, use **equivalent fractions** with like denominators. You can use **common denominators** of two or more fractions to write equivalent fractions. A common denominator is a **common multiple** of two or more denominators.

Example 1

Sani makes a fruit salad by combining $\frac{1}{2}$ cup apples and $\frac{1}{4}$ cup peaches. What is the total amount of fruit in Sani's fruit salad?

Strategy   Use equivalent fractions with like denominators.

Step 1   Find a common denominator of $\frac{1}{2}$ and $\frac{1}{4}$.

4 is a multiple of 2 and 4. 4 is a common denominator.

Step 2   Write equivalent fractions using the common denominator.

Multiply the numerator by the same number.

$\frac{1}{2} = \frac{1 \times 2}{2 \times 2} = \frac{2}{4}$

$\frac{1}{4}$ already has a denominator of 4.

Step 3   Add the fractions with like denominators.

$\frac{1}{2} + \frac{1}{4} = \frac{2}{4} + \frac{1}{4} = \frac{3}{4}$

Step 4 Use fraction strips to check the sum.

$\frac{1}{2}$	$\frac{1}{4}$

$\frac{1}{4}$	$\frac{1}{4}$	$\frac{1}{4}$

The model shows that $\frac{1}{2} + \frac{1}{4} = \frac{1}{4} + \frac{1}{4} + \frac{1}{4} = \frac{3}{4}$.

Solution Sani's fruit salad has a total of $\frac{3}{4}$ cup of fruit.

You can also write the sum of three fractions with unlike denominators using equivalent fractions with like denominators.

Example 2

Add $\frac{1}{6} + \frac{1}{4} + \frac{1}{3}$.

Strategy Use equivalent fractions with like denominators.

Step 1 Find a common denominator.

Find multiples of the greatest denominator, 6.

Multiples of 6: 6, 12, 18, 24, . . .

Find the least multiple that is also a multiple of 4 and 3.

12 is a multiple of both 4 and 3. 12 is a common denominator.

Step 2 Write equivalent fractions using the common denominator.

Multiply the numerator and denominator by a factor that makes the denominator equal to 12.

$$\frac{1}{6} = \frac{1 \times 2}{6 \times 2} = \frac{2}{12}$$

$$\frac{1}{4} = \frac{1 \times 3}{4 \times 3} = \frac{3}{12}$$

$$\frac{1}{3} = \frac{1 \times 4}{3 \times 4} = \frac{4}{12}$$

Step 3 Add the fractions with like denominators.

$$\frac{1}{6} + \frac{1}{4} + \frac{1}{3} = \frac{2}{12} + \frac{3}{12} + \frac{4}{12}$$

$$= \frac{9}{12}$$

Step 4 Simplify.

$$\frac{9}{12} = \frac{9 \div 3}{12 \div 3} = \frac{3}{4}$$

Step 5 Use fraction strips to check the sum.

The model shows that

$$\frac{1}{6} + \frac{1}{4} + \frac{1}{3} = \frac{2}{12} + \frac{3}{12} + \frac{4}{12} = \frac{9}{12}.$$

$\frac{1}{6}$	$\frac{1}{4}$	$\frac{1}{3}$	

$\frac{1}{12}$	$\frac{1}{12}$	$\frac{1}{12}$	$\frac{1}{12}$	$\frac{1}{12}$	$\frac{1}{12}$	$\frac{1}{12}$	$\frac{1}{12}$	$\frac{1}{12}$	

Solution $\frac{1}{6} + \frac{1}{4} + \frac{1}{3} = \frac{9}{12}$, or $\frac{3}{4}$

Example 3

Add $2\frac{2}{5} + 4\frac{2}{3}$.

Strategy Find a common denominator for the fraction parts.

Step 1 Find a common denominator.

You can multiply the denominators to find a common denominator.

$5 \times 3 = 15$

Step 2 Write equivalent fractions using the common denominator.

$$\frac{2}{5} = \frac{2 \times 3}{5 \times 3} = \frac{6}{15}$$

$$\frac{2}{3} = \frac{2 \times 5}{3 \times 5} = \frac{10}{15}$$

Step 3 Rewrite the mixed numbers using the common denominator.

$$2\frac{2}{5} = 2\frac{6}{15} \qquad 4\frac{2}{3} = 4\frac{10}{15}$$

Step 4 Regroup the mixed numbers as the sum of the whole number parts and the fraction parts.

$$2\frac{2}{5} + 4\frac{2}{3} = 2\frac{6}{15} + 4\frac{10}{15}$$

$$= \left(2 + \frac{6}{15}\right) + \left(4 + \frac{10}{15}\right)$$

$$= (2 + 4) + \left(\frac{6}{15} + \frac{10}{15}\right)$$

Step 5 Add the whole number parts. Add the fraction parts. Simplify.

$$(2 + 4) + \left(\frac{6}{15} + \frac{10}{15}\right) = 6 + \frac{16}{15}$$

$$= 6 + \frac{15}{15} + \frac{1}{15}$$

$$= 6 + 1 + \frac{1}{15}$$

$$= 7 + \frac{1}{15}$$

Solution $2\frac{2}{5} + 4\frac{2}{3} = 7\frac{1}{15}$

Example 4

Subtract $\frac{5}{6} - \frac{1}{8}$.

Strategy   Use equivalent fractions with like denominators.

Step 1   Find a common denominator.

Make a list of multiples of the greater denominator, 8.

Multiples of 8: 8, 16, 24, 32, 40, . . .

Find the least multiple that is also a multiple of 6.

24 is a multiple of 6. 24 is a common denominator.

Step 2   Write equivalent fractions with the common denominator.

$$\frac{5}{6} = \frac{5 \times 4}{6 \times 4} = \frac{20}{24}$$

$$\frac{1}{8} = \frac{1 \times 3}{8 \times 3} = \frac{3}{24}$$

Step 3   Subtract the fractions with like denominators.

$$\frac{5}{6} - \frac{1}{8} = \frac{20}{24} - \frac{3}{24}$$
$$= \frac{17}{24}$$

Step 4   Use addition to check your answer.

$$\frac{17}{24} + \frac{3}{24} = \frac{20}{24} \text{ or } \frac{5}{6} \checkmark$$

Step 5   Model the difference.

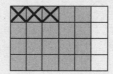

The model shows $\frac{5}{6}$ of the rectangle shaded.

20 out of 24 parts are shaded, so $\frac{20}{24}$ is shaded.

3 parts, or $\frac{1}{8}$ of the rectangle, are subtracted, with 17 shaded parts remaining.

$$\frac{5}{6} - \frac{1}{8} = \frac{17}{24}$$

Solution $\frac{5}{6} - \frac{1}{8} = \frac{17}{24}$

Sometimes when you subtract mixed numbers, you may need to change the mixed numbers to **improper fractions**. To change a mixed number to an improper fraction, first multiply the denominator and the whole number, then add the numerator. This gives the numerator of the improper fraction. The denominator of the improper fraction is the same as the fraction part of the mixed number.

$$2\frac{3}{5} = \frac{5 \times 2 + 3}{5} = \frac{13}{5}$$

Example 5

Subtract $2\frac{7}{10} - 1\frac{1}{4}$.

Strategy   Change the mixed numbers to improper fractions. Then use equivalent fractions to find the difference.

Step 1   Write the mixed numbers as improper fractions.

$$2\frac{7}{10} = \frac{10 \times 2 + 7}{10} = \frac{27}{10}$$
$$1\frac{1}{4} = \frac{4 \times 1 + 1}{4} = \frac{5}{4}$$

Step 2   Find a common denominator.

Make a list of multiples of the greater denominator, 10.

Multiples of 10: 10, 20, 30, 40, 50, . . .

20 is the least multiple that is also a multiple of 4.

Therefore, 20 is a common denominator.

Step 3   Write equivalent fractions with common denominators.

$$\frac{27}{10} = \frac{27 \times 2}{10 \times 2} = \frac{54}{20}$$
$$\frac{5}{4} = \frac{5 \times 5}{4 \times 5} = \frac{25}{20}$$

Step 4   Find the difference.

$$\frac{27}{10} - \frac{5}{4} = \frac{54}{20} - \frac{25}{20}$$
$$= \frac{29}{20}$$

Write the improper fraction as a mixed number.

$$\frac{29}{20} = 29 \div 20 = 1\text{ R}9 = 1\frac{9}{20}$$

Step 5   Use addition to check your answer.

$$\frac{29}{20} + \frac{25}{20} = \frac{54}{20} = 2\frac{14}{20} = 2\frac{7}{10} \checkmark$$

Solution $2\frac{7}{10} - 1\frac{1}{4} = 1\frac{9}{20}$

Find $\frac{1}{6} + \frac{5}{8} - \frac{2}{3}$.

Find a common denominator.

Make a list of multiples of the greatest denominator, 8.

    Multiples of 8: _____

    Find the least multiple of 8 that is also a multiple of 3 and 6. _____

Write equivalent fractions with common denominators.

$$\frac{1}{6} = \frac{\boxed{} \times \boxed{}}{\boxed{} \times \boxed{}} = \frac{\boxed{}}{\boxed{}}$$

$$\frac{5}{8} = \frac{\boxed{} \times \boxed{}}{\boxed{} \times \boxed{}} = \frac{\boxed{}}{\boxed{}}$$

$$\frac{2}{3} = \frac{\boxed{} \times \boxed{}}{\boxed{} \times \boxed{}} = \frac{\boxed{}}{\boxed{}}$$

Rewrite $\frac{1}{6} + \frac{5}{8} - \frac{2}{3}$ using common denominators, and find the answer.

$$\frac{1}{6} + \frac{5}{8} - \frac{2}{3} = \frac{\boxed{}}{\boxed{}} + \frac{\boxed{}}{\boxed{}} - \frac{\boxed{}}{\boxed{}}$$

$$= \frac{\boxed{}}{\boxed{}} - \frac{\boxed{}}{\boxed{}}$$

$$= \frac{\boxed{}}{\boxed{}}$$

Simplify.

$$= \frac{\boxed{}}{\boxed{}}$$

$$\frac{1}{6} + \frac{5}{8} - \frac{2}{3} = \frac{\boxed{}}{\boxed{}}$$

1 Tim walked $\frac{3}{10}$ mile to the post office. Then he walked $\frac{1}{5}$ mile to the gym. How far did Tim walk all together? Draw fraction strips to model the total number of miles Tim walked. Then draw fraction strips to show equivalent fractions with a common denominator. Find the sum.

Tim walked _____ miles all together.

2 Use numbers from the box to find equivalent fractions and the sum.

$$\frac{1}{3} + \frac{1}{6} + \frac{1}{12} = \underline{\hspace{1cm}} + \underline{\hspace{1cm}} + \underline{\hspace{1cm}} = \underline{\hspace{1cm}}$$

$\frac{1}{12}$	$\frac{5}{12}$
$\frac{2}{12}$	$\frac{6}{12}$
$\frac{3}{12}$	$\frac{7}{12}$
$\frac{4}{12}$	$\frac{8}{12}$

3 Compare each sum or difference to 1 whole. Write the problem in the correct box.

$1\frac{5}{6} - \frac{5}{12}$	$1\frac{1}{10} - \frac{1}{5}$	$1\frac{3}{6} - \frac{3}{4}$	$\frac{9}{10} + \frac{1}{5}$	$\frac{7}{9} + \frac{1}{4}$	$\frac{4}{7} + \frac{1}{3}$

Less than 1	Greater than 1

4 Select True or False for each equation.

A. $\frac{1}{2} + \frac{3}{4} = 1\frac{12}{16}$ ○ True   ○ False

B. $1\frac{5}{6} - \frac{1}{3} = 1\frac{3}{6}$ ○ True   ○ False

C. $\frac{3}{5} - \frac{1}{2} = \frac{2}{3}$ ○ True   ○ False

D. $\frac{8}{10} + \frac{1}{3} = 1\frac{2}{15}$ ○ True   ○ False

5 Which problem has a sum or difference of $\frac{7}{12}$? Circle all that apply.

A. $\frac{3}{4} + \frac{1}{6}$ **D.** $\frac{1}{4} + \frac{1}{6} + \frac{1}{12}$

B. $\frac{3}{4} - \frac{1}{6}$ **E.** $\frac{2}{3} - \frac{1}{12}$

C. $\frac{1}{3} + \frac{1}{4}$ **F.** $\frac{2}{3} + \frac{1}{6}$

6 Circle the number that makes each equation true.

$$\frac{4}{5} - \boxed{\begin{array}{c} \frac{1}{3} \\ \frac{1}{2} \\ \frac{2}{3} \end{array}} = \frac{2}{15} \qquad\qquad 1\frac{5}{8} + \boxed{\begin{array}{c} 2\frac{5}{6} \\ 3\frac{2}{3} \\ 4\frac{2}{3} \end{array}} = 5\frac{7}{24}$$

7 The table shows the amount of time Luis practiced his trumpet last week.

Day of Week	Monday	Wednesday	Thursday
Time (hours)	$1\frac{1}{3}$	$2\frac{1}{2}$	$1\frac{3}{4}$

Part A

Luis wants to find the total time he spent practicing. What is the first step he should take to add the times?

Part B

Find the total number of hours Luis practiced his trumpet. Show your work.

8 Barid says that $\frac{1}{2} + \frac{1}{3}$ equals $\frac{2}{6}$. What mistake did Barid make?

9 Lamar needs to find the sum of $\frac{3}{6}$ and $\frac{2}{3}$. Could he multiply the denominators to find a common denominator? Explain why he may or may not want to do this.

10 Duval had $\frac{7}{8}$ quart of milk. He used $\frac{1}{6}$ quart for a recipe.

Part A

How much milk does Duval have left? Show your work.

Part B

Explain how you can check your answer.

11 Find the value of $\frac{5}{8} + \frac{2}{3} - \frac{1}{4}$. Use words, numbers, or models to justify your answer.

Solving Problems with Addition and Subtraction of Fractions

You can write **equations** and use models to add and subtract fractions in word problems.

For example, the model below shows a snack made of $\frac{1}{2}$ cup almonds and $\frac{2}{5}$ cup cranberries.

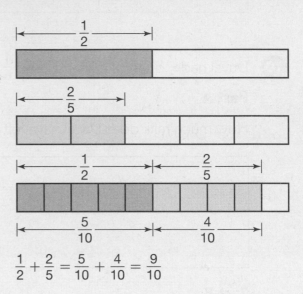

$$\frac{1}{2} + \frac{2}{5} = \frac{5}{10} + \frac{4}{10} = \frac{9}{10}$$

Example 1

Ben makes a sauce by combining $\frac{2}{3}$ cup tomatoes with $\frac{1}{4}$ cup lime juice. How much sauce does Ben make?

Strategy   Determine the operation needed to solve the problem. Write an equation.

Step 1   Write an equation.

You can add to find a total amount after combining ingredients.

$$\frac{2}{3} + \frac{1}{4} = \boxed{}$$

Step 2   Write equivalent fractions using a common denominator.

A common denominator of $\frac{2}{3}$ and $\frac{1}{4}$ is 12.

$$\frac{2}{3} = \frac{2 \times 4}{3 \times 4} = \frac{8}{12} \qquad\qquad \frac{1}{4} = \frac{1 \times 3}{4 \times 3} = \frac{3}{12}$$

Step 3   Add the fractions with like denominators.

$$\frac{2}{3} + \frac{1}{4} = \frac{8}{12} + \frac{3}{12} = \frac{11}{12}$$

Step 4	Use a model to check your answer.

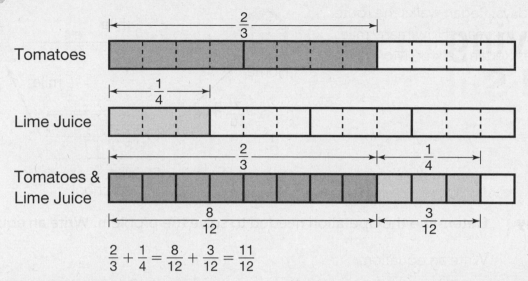

$$\frac{2}{3} + \frac{1}{4} = \frac{8}{12} + \frac{3}{12} = \frac{11}{12}$$

Solution Ben makes $\frac{11}{12}$ cup of sauce.

Example 2

Lela bought $\frac{4}{5}$ yard of fabric to use on projects. She used $\frac{1}{4}$ yard on her first project. How much fabric does Lela have left?

Strategy Determine the operation needed to solve the problem. Write an equation.

Step 1	Write an equation.

You want to find out how much fabric is left after Lela uses some.

Subtract to find out how much remains after some is taken away.

$$\frac{4}{5} - \frac{1}{4} = \boxed{}$$

Step 2	Write equivalent fractions using a common denominator.

A common denominator of $\frac{4}{5}$ and $\frac{1}{4}$ is 20.

$$\frac{4}{5} = \frac{4 \times 4}{5 \times 4} = \frac{16}{20} \qquad \frac{1}{4} = \frac{1 \times 5}{4 \times 5} = \frac{5}{20}$$

Step 3	Subtract the fractions with like denominators.

$$\frac{4}{5} - \frac{1}{4} = \frac{16}{20} - \frac{5}{20} = \frac{11}{20}$$

Step 4	Use addition to check your answer.

$$\frac{11}{20} + \frac{5}{20} = \frac{16}{20} \text{ or } \frac{4}{5} \checkmark$$

Solution Lela has $\frac{11}{20}$ yard of fabric left.

Example 3

On Mondays, Regan walks the route shown on the map. How many miles in all does Regan walk on Mondays?

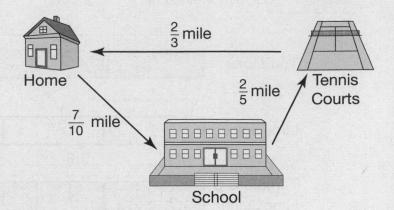

Home

$\frac{2}{3}$ mile

Tennis Courts

$\frac{2}{5}$ mile

$\frac{7}{10}$ mile

School

Strategy Determine the operation needed to solve the problem. Write an equation.

Step 1 Write an equation.

The three distances are shown on the map. Add to find the total.

$$\frac{7}{10} + \frac{2}{5} + \frac{2}{3} = \boxed{}$$

Step 2 Write equivalent fractions using a common denominator.

A common denominator of $\frac{7}{10}$, $\frac{2}{5}$, and $\frac{2}{3}$ is 30.

$$\frac{7}{10} = \frac{21}{30} \qquad \frac{2}{5} = \frac{12}{30} \qquad \frac{2}{3} = \frac{20}{30}$$

Step 3 Add the fractions with like denominators.

$$\frac{7}{10} + \frac{2}{5} + \frac{2}{3} = \frac{21}{30} + \frac{12}{30} + \frac{20}{30} = \frac{53}{30}, \text{ or } 1\frac{23}{30}$$

Step 4 Use benchmark fractions to determine if your answer is reasonable.

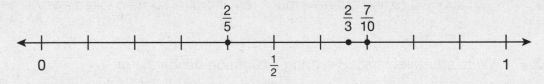

All three fractions are closer to $\frac{1}{2}$ than to 0 or 1. Estimate the sum.

$$\frac{1}{2} + \frac{1}{2} + \frac{1}{2} = 1\frac{1}{2}. \leftarrow \text{This is close to } 1\frac{23}{30}. \text{ The answer is reasonable.}$$

Solution Regan walks $1\frac{23}{30}$ miles in all on Mondays.

Jake and Paco each ordered a small pizza. Jake ate $\frac{7}{8}$ of his pizza. Paco ate $\frac{2}{3}$ of his pizza. How much more pizza did Jake eat than Paco?

Write an equation.

To find how much more, which operation should you use? _____

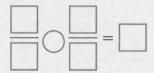

Write equivalent fractions with a common denominator.

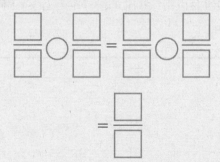

_____ the fractions with like denominators. Solve.

$$\frac{\square}{\square} \bigcirc \frac{\square}{\square} = \frac{\square}{\square} \bigcirc \frac{\square}{\square}$$

$$= \frac{\square}{\square}$$

Use benchmark fractions to determine if your answer is reasonable.

Is each fraction closer to 0, $\frac{1}{2}$, or 1?

Estimate: $\frac{7}{8}$ is closer to _____.

$\frac{2}{3}$ is closer to _____.

Estimate the answer. _____

Explain how you know your exact answer is reasonable.

_____

_____

Jake ate _____ more pizza than Paco.

3 LESSON PRACTICE

1 On Saturday, Ana worked $\frac{1}{4}$ of a day washing cars for a fund-raiser. On Sunday, she worked $\frac{1}{3}$ of a day babysitting. What part of a day did she work on Saturday and Sunday? Draw and label the bars to represent the situation.

Write an equation to represent the model. _____

Ana worked _____ of a day on Saturday and Sunday.

2 Meg bought two pieces of ribbon to decorate a picture frame. One piece was $\frac{3}{5}$ yard long. The other piece was $\frac{1}{2}$ yard long. What is the total length of ribbon Meg bought? Use words, pictures, or numbers to justify your answer.

3 Inez has $\frac{3}{5}$ quart of orange juice. She drank $\frac{1}{3}$ quart. How much orange juice does she now have? Explain how you know your answer is reasonable.

4 Nikko combined raisins, nuts, and granola to make $1\frac{3}{4}$ cups of snacks. Use numbers from the box to complete two different equations that Nikko could have used to find a sum of $1\frac{3}{4}$ cups.

$$1\frac{3}{4} = \underline{\hspace{1cm}} + \underline{\hspace{1cm}} + \underline{\hspace{1cm}}$$

$$1\frac{3}{4} = \underline{\hspace{1cm}} + \underline{\hspace{1cm}} + \underline{\hspace{1cm}}$$

1	$\frac{1}{8}$
$\frac{1}{4}$	$\frac{2}{3}$
$\frac{1}{2}$	$\frac{1}{12}$

5 Nana wants to paint her bedroom walls light blue. She will mix white and blue paint to get the shade she wants. Which expression has the same value as a mixture of $\frac{3}{8}$ gallon blue paint with $\frac{1}{2}$ gallon white paint? Circle all that apply.

A. $\frac{5}{8} + \frac{1}{4}$ **E.** $\frac{3}{8} + \frac{1}{2}$

B. $\frac{3}{4} + \frac{1}{8}$ **F.** $\frac{3}{8} + \frac{4}{24}$

C. $\frac{1}{8} + \frac{5}{8}$ **G.** $\frac{5}{8} + \frac{4}{16}$

D. $\frac{1}{4} + \frac{1}{8}$ **H.** $\frac{3}{4} + \frac{6}{12}$

6 Kade makes $\frac{5}{6}$ cup salad dressing. He uses $\frac{2}{3}$ cup dressing on a salad. How much salad dressing is left?

Write an equation to represent the situation using a common denominator.

_____

Kade has _____ cup salad dressing left.

7 The table shows the ingredients, in cups, that Rosa used in her smoothie recipe.

Berry Delicious Smoothie

Mixed Berries	Yogurt	Milk
$2\frac{1}{2}$	$1\frac{1}{3}$	$1\frac{1}{4}$

Part A

Write each mixed number as an improper fraction. Find a common denominator. Then write equivalent fractions for the improper fractions. Show your work.

$2\frac{1}{2} = $ _____ $ = $ _____

$1\frac{1}{3} = $ _____ $ = $ _____

$1\frac{1}{4} = $ _____ $ = $ _____

Part B

Find the total number of cups of ingredients in Rosa's smoothie. Show your work.

8 Dion grated $\frac{1}{2}$ cup of cheese for a pasta dish. The recipe calls for $\frac{2}{3}$ cup. How much more cheese does Dion need to grate? Which equation could Dion have written to correctly solve his problem? Circle all that apply.

A. $\frac{2}{3} = \frac{1}{2} + \frac{1}{3}$

B. $\frac{2}{3} - \frac{1}{2} = \frac{4}{6} - \frac{3}{6}$

C. $\frac{2}{3} - \frac{1}{2} = \frac{8}{12} - \frac{6}{12}$

D. $\frac{2}{3} + \frac{1}{2} = \frac{4}{6} + \frac{3}{6}$

9 Kate is planting a garden. She will plant $\frac{3}{10}$ of her garden with herbs, and $\frac{3}{5}$ of her garden will be vegetables. She will plant flowers in the rest of her garden. Select True or False for each statement.

A. $\frac{1}{5}$ of Kate's garden is flowers. ○ True ○ False

B. $\frac{9}{10}$ of Kate's garden is herbs and vegetables. ○ True ○ False

C. $\frac{7}{10}$ of Kate's garden is flowers and vegetables. ○ True ○ False

D. $\frac{3}{10}$ of Kate's garden is flowers and herbs. ○ True ○ False

10 Yuri made a fruit salad with $\frac{1}{3}$ cup blueberries, $\frac{5}{8}$ cup strawberries, and $\frac{5}{6}$ cup apples.

Part A

How much fruit salad did Yuri make?

Part B

Use benchmark fractions to determine if your answer is reasonable. Show your work.

Part C

Explain how to determine if your estimate for $\frac{1}{3} + \frac{5}{8} + \frac{5}{6}$ is greater than the actual sum.

Interpreting Fractions as Division

A fraction represents division of the numerator by the denominator. So, any fraction can be written as a division expression.

dividend → $\frac{2}{5}$ ← divisor

dividend ↓

$2 \div 5$

↑ divisor

Example 1

Divide $3 \div 4$.

Strategy   Use a model.

Step 1   Model the division expression.

$3 \div 4$ means to divide 3 objects equally into 4 groups. There are not enough whole objects to divide into 4 groups. So, divide each whole into 4 parts.

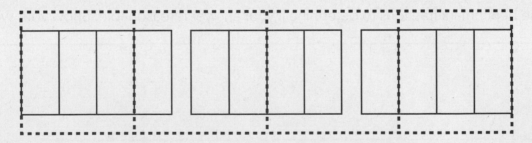

Step 2   Write the quotient.

Each whole has 4 parts. There are 3 parts in each group. So, the fraction $\frac{3}{4}$ represents the quotient.

Solution $3 \div 4 = \frac{3}{4}$

Example 2

Shawn has 2 granola bars. He wants to share them equally among himself, Justin, and Luisana. How much will each person receive?

Strategy   Write an equation and use a model.

Step 1   Write an equation to model the problem.

There are 2 granola bars being divided among 3 people. This can be represented as $2 \div 3 = \boxed{}$.

Step 2   Use models to find the quotient.

Because there are 3 people, divide each whole into 3 parts. Count how many parts each person receives.

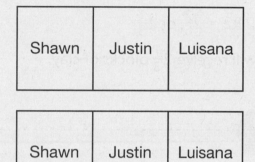

Each person can have 2 one-third pieces of a granola bar. So, each person receives $\frac{2}{3}$ of a whole bar.

$2 \div 3 = \frac{2}{3}$

Solution   Each person will receive $\frac{2}{3}$ of a granola bar.

Example 3

There are 6 students in Mrs. Martin's class who want to use clay for their art projects. Mrs. Martin has 14 blocks of clay. If the students divide the clay equally, how much clay will each student receive?

Strategy   Write an equation and use a model.

Step 1   Write an equation to model the problem.

There are 14 blocks of clay being divided among 6 students. This can be represented as $14 \div 6 = \boxed{}$.

Step 2   Divide.

$$14 \div 6 = 2\ R2$$

Step 3   Determine an approximate result.

14 blocks of clay are being shared among 6 students.

Each student can have 2 whole blocks of clay, because $6 \times 2 = 12$.

Each student cannot have 3 whole blocks because $6 \times 3 = 18$.

Each student will receive between 2 and 3 blocks of clay.

Step 4   Write the quotient as a mixed number.

The quotient is the whole number part of the mixed number.

The remainder is the numerator of the fraction part of the mixed number.

The divisor is the denominator of the fraction part of the mixed number.

$$14 \div 6 = 2\ R2 = 2\frac{2}{6},\ \text{or } 2\frac{1}{3}$$

Solution   Each student will receive $2\frac{1}{3}$ blocks of clay.

② COACHED EXAMPLE ---

A zookeeper has a 30-gallon tank of water. She divides the water equally among 12 animals. How many gallons of water does each animal get?

Write an equation to model the problem.

_____ ÷ _____ = ☐

Divide. _____ ÷ _____ = _____ R _____

Determine an approximate result. Between which two whole numbers does the answer lie?

_____ and _____

Write the quotient as a mixed number. _____

Each animal gets _____ gallons of water.

1 Draw a line from each division problem to its quotient.

A. $5 \div 6$ •   • $1\frac{1}{5}$

B. $6 \div 5$ •   • $\frac{2}{5}$

C. $16 \div 40$ •   • $\frac{5}{6}$

D. $40 \div 16$ •   • $2\frac{1}{2}$

2 Elly has 3 pounds of turkey to make 12 sandwiches. She puts the same amount of turkey on each sandwich. Select True or False for each statement.

A. Each sandwich has more than 1 pound of turkey.   ○ True ○ False

B. Each sandwich has $12 \div 3$ pounds of turkey.   ○ True ○ False

C. Elly can put $\frac{1}{4}$ pound of turkey on each sandwich.   ○ True ○ False

D. Elly will have $\frac{1}{2}$ pound of turkey left over.   ○ True ○ False

3 Circle the numbers that make the equations true.

| 5 |
| 15 |
| 23 |

$11 \div \boxed{15} = 2\frac{1}{5}$

| 9 |
| 12 |
| 20 |

$\boxed{12} \div 16 = \frac{3}{4}$

4 Look at the division problem. Is the quotient equal to $1\frac{1}{2}$? Select Yes or No.

A. $3 \div 6$ ○ Yes   ○ No

B. $5 \div 2$ ○ Yes   ○ No

C. $12 \div 8$ ○ Yes   ○ No

D. $16 \div 24$ ○ Yes   ○ No

5 Compare each quotient to 2. Write the problem in the correct box.

| $7 \div 8$ | $12 \div 5$ | $30 \div 18$ | $14 \div 35$ | $7 \div 2$ | $30 \div 20$ |

Less than 2	Greater than 2

6 Use numbers from the box to complete the equations.

$$3 \div 8 = \frac{\square}{\square}$$

$$6 \div 15 = \frac{\square}{5}$$

$$10 \div \underline{\hspace{1cm}} = 2\frac{1}{2}$$

| 2 |
| 3 |
| 4 |
| 8 |
| 12 |

7 Miguel and 2 of his friends share 7 rice cakes equally. Select an equation that represents how much each person receives. Circle all that apply.

A. $2 \div 7 = \frac{2}{7}$

B. $3 \div 7 = \frac{3}{7}$

C. $7 \div 2 = 3\frac{1}{2}$

D. $7 \div 3 = \frac{7}{3}$

E. $7 \div 3 = 2\frac{1}{3}$

F. $7 \div 3 = 3\frac{1}{2}$

8 Anna has 5 dog treats that she wants to share equally among 3 dogs.

Part A

Draw a model to show how much each dog will get.

Part B

Write an equation to represent the problem.

_____

Part C

How much does each dog get? Explain how you found your answer.

9 A basketball coach has 40 ounces of sunflower seeds. She wants to divide the seeds equally into 12 bags to give to her players after the game.

Each player will receive between _____ and _____ ounces of sunflower seeds.

What is the exact amount of sunflower seeds each player will receive? Write your answer as a mixed number.

_____ ounces

10 Write the division problem in the correct box to show the location of its quotient on the number line.

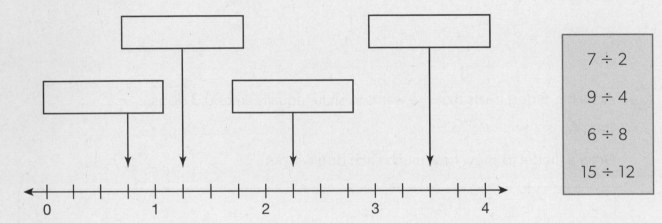

11 Marcus and Beth are organizing a party. They plan to serve pudding for dessert. Marcus thinks they should make 5 cups of pudding for every 3 people. Beth thinks they should make 6 cups of pudding for every 4 people. The pudding will be divided equally into dessert bowls.

Will each person get more pudding under Marcus's plan or Beth's plan? _____

Use words, numbers, or models to justify your answer.

Multiplying Fractions

1 GETTING THE IDEA

To multiply fractions, multiply the numerators and multiply the denominators.

$$\frac{3}{5} \times \frac{7}{8} = \frac{3 \times 7}{5 \times 8}$$ ← Multiply the numerators.
← Multiply the denominators.

$$= \frac{21}{40}$$

To multiply a whole number by a fraction, you can write the whole number as a fraction. Then multiply as you would with fractions.

Example 1

Multiply $5 \times \frac{2}{3}$.

Strategy Write the whole number as a fraction. Multiply the numerators and the denominators.

Step 1 Model the multiplication problem.

$5 \times \frac{2}{3}$ means 5 groups of $\frac{2}{3}$.

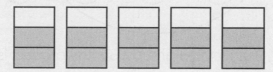

10 parts or $\frac{10}{3}$ are shaded. So, the product is $\frac{10}{3}$ or $3\frac{1}{3}$.

Step 2 Write the whole number as a fraction.

Write 5 as $\frac{5}{1}$.

$$5 \times \frac{2}{3} = \frac{5}{1} \times \frac{2}{3}$$

Step 3 Multiply the numerators and then the denominators.

$$\frac{5}{1} \times \frac{2}{3} = \frac{5 \times 2}{1 \times 3} = \frac{10}{3}$$

Write the improper fraction as a mixed number.

$$\frac{10}{3} = 10 \div 3 = 3\,R1$$

$$\frac{10}{3} = 3\frac{1}{3}$$

Solution $5 \times \frac{2}{3} = 3\frac{1}{3}$

Example 2

Multiply $\frac{3}{4} \times 12$.

Strategy   **Write the whole number as a fraction. Multiply the numerators and the denominators.**

Step 1   Model the multiplication problem.

$\frac{3}{4} \times 12$ means $\frac{3}{4}$ of 12.

Draw 12 circles. Arrange the 12 circles into 4 equal groups. Circle 3 groups.

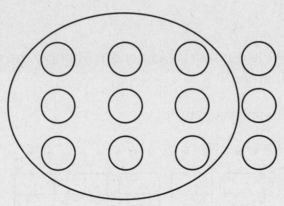

There are 9 circles in 3 groups. So, the product is 9.

Step 2   Write the whole number as a fraction.

Write 12 as $\frac{12}{1}$.

$$\frac{3}{4} \times 12 = \frac{3}{4} \times \frac{12}{1}$$

Step 3   Multiply the numerators and then the denominators.

$$\frac{3}{4} \times \frac{12}{1} = \frac{3 \times 12}{4 \times 1} = \frac{36}{4}$$

Step 4 Write the improper fraction as a whole number.

$$\frac{36}{4} = 36 \div 4 = 9$$

$$\frac{36}{4} = 9$$

Solution $\frac{3}{4} \times 12 = 9$

Example 3

Write and solve a word problem for $4 \times \frac{3}{8}$.

Strategy   **Use models to represent the problem.**

Step 1   Determine what the numbers will represent.

Multiplication can be used to represent joining equal-sized objects. The whole number can represent the number of objects. The fraction can represent the size of one object.

Step 2   Make a model.

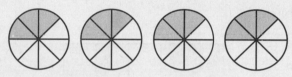

The model shows 4 circles. Each circle has $\frac{3}{8}$ shaded.

Step 3   Write a word problem.

Justin puts 4 oranges in a bag. Each orange weighs $\frac{3}{8}$ pound. How much does the bag of oranges weigh?

Step 4   Solve the problem.

$$4 \times \frac{3}{8} = \frac{4}{1} \times \frac{3}{8} = \frac{4 \times 3}{1 \times 8} = \frac{12}{8}$$

$$\frac{12}{8} = 12 \div 8 = 1\ R4$$

$$\frac{12}{8} = 1\frac{4}{8} \text{ or } 1\frac{1}{2}$$

The model shows that 12 parts are shaded.

$$\frac{12}{8} = 1\frac{1}{2}$$

Solution   **Justin puts 4 oranges in a bag. Each orange weighs $\frac{3}{8}$ pound. How much does the bag of oranges weigh? The bag of oranges weighs $1\frac{1}{2}$ pounds.**

Example 4

Multiply $\frac{2}{5} \times \frac{1}{3}$.

Strategy   **Model the problem. Then multiply the numerators and denominators.**

> **Step 1**   Draw a diagram to model the problem.

The first factor is $\frac{2}{5}$, so make a model showing 5 equal parts with 2 parts shaded.

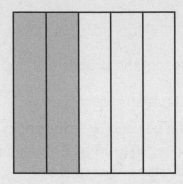

The second factor is $\frac{1}{3}$, so divide the same model into 3 equal parts with 1 part shaded.

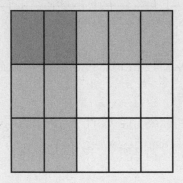

The parts of the model that were shaded twice represent the product.

2 parts out of 15 are shaded twice. So, $\frac{2}{5}$ of $\frac{1}{3}$ is $\frac{2}{15}$.

> **Step 2**   Multiply to find the product.

Multiply the numerators and then the denominators.

$$\frac{2}{5} \times \frac{1}{3} = \frac{2 \times 1}{5 \times 3} = \frac{2}{15}$$

Solution $\frac{2}{5} \times \frac{1}{3} = \frac{2}{15}$

Create and solve a problem for $\frac{1}{4} \times \frac{1}{2}$.

Determine what the numbers will represent.

_____

_____

Draw a diagram to model the problem.

   The first factor is _____, so make a model showing _____ equal parts with _____ part(s) shaded.

   The second factor is _____, so divide the same model into _____ equal parts with _____ part(s) shaded.

   The parts of the model that are shaded twice show the _____.

   What part of the model is shaded twice? _____

Write a word problem.

_____

_____

_____

The answer to the word problem is _____.

1 Write a multiplication equation for the model.

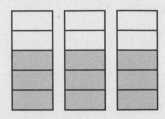

_____

2 Draw a line from each multiplication problem to its product.

A. $2 \times \frac{5}{8}$ •

B. $\frac{3}{8} \times \frac{1}{2}$ •

C. $\frac{5}{6} \times \frac{3}{5}$ •

D. $\frac{7}{12} \times 3$ •

• $1\frac{1}{4}$

• $\frac{1}{2}$

• $1\frac{3}{4}$

• $\frac{3}{16}$

3 Jayna has 4 feet of string to make toys for her cats. She wants to use the same amount of string for each toy. Does she have enough string to make the following toys? Circle all that apply.

A. 3 toys that each use $\frac{3}{4}$ foot of string

B. 4 toys that each use $\frac{11}{12}$ foot of string

C. 5 toys that each use $\frac{4}{5}$ foot of string

D. 5 toys that each use $\frac{7}{8}$ foot of string

E. 6 toys that each use $\frac{2}{3}$ foot of string

F. 6 toys that each use $\frac{5}{6}$ foot of sting

4 Dustin is making bran muffins. The table shows some of the ingredients needed for 1 batch of muffins.

Ingredients	Raisins	Buttermilk	Brown Sugar	Flour
Amount	$\frac{1}{2}$ cup	$\frac{3}{4}$ cup	$\frac{3}{4}$ cup	1 cup

Part A

The amount of wheat bran is 3 times the amount of raisins. How much wheat bran is used in the recipe?

_____ cup(s)

Part B

The amount of vegetable oil is $\frac{1}{2}$ the amount of brown sugar. How much vegetable oil is used in the recipe?

_____ cup(s)

Part C

Dustin has 3 cups of buttermilk. Does he have enough to make 4 batches of muffins? Explain.

5 Compare each product to 1. Write the multiplication problem in the correct box.

$3 \times \frac{1}{2}$	$\frac{3}{5} \times \frac{5}{3}$	$5 \times \frac{1}{4}$	$\frac{4}{3} \times \frac{2}{5}$	$\frac{1}{10} \times 9$	$\frac{1}{8} \times 8$

Less than 1	Equal to 1	Greater than 1

6 On a fruit farm, $\frac{1}{2}$ of the trees are apple trees and $\frac{1}{4}$ are pear trees. The rest of the trees are peach trees. Out of the apple trees, $\frac{2}{3}$ of the trees have red apples and the rest have green apples. There are 60 trees in all. Select True or False for each statement.

A. $\frac{1}{3}$ of the trees on the farm have red apples.   ○ True   ○ False

B. $\frac{1}{6}$ of the trees on the farm have green apples.   ○ True   ○ False

C. There are 25 pear trees.   ○ True   ○ False

D. There are 15 peach trees.   ○ True   ○ False

7 Create and solve a problem for $\frac{5}{6} \times 12$.

8 There is $\frac{1}{3}$ of a container of juice left. Alicia drinks $\frac{1}{2}$ of the juice that is left.

Part A

Draw a model to represent the problem.

Part B

Write and solve an equation for the model.

Area of Rectangles

1 GETTING THE IDEA

A **unit square** has side lengths of 1 unit and an area of 1 square unit.

You can divide a unit square into smaller squares with fractional side lengths.

The side lengths of the unit square below have been divided into fourths, so each of the smaller squares has a side length of $\frac{1}{4}$ unit.

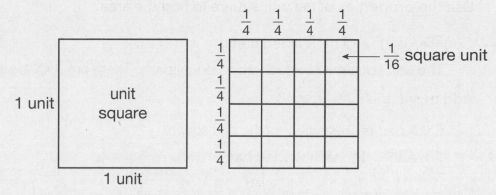

Each small square represents $\frac{1}{16}$ of the unit square. So, the area of each small square is $\frac{1}{16}$ square unit.

You can find the area of a rectangle by counting square units. You can also find the area by the formula for the area.

Area = length × width

$A = l \times w$

Example 1

The shaded rectangle has a length of $\frac{2}{3}$ unit and a width of $\frac{4}{5}$ unit. Find the area of the rectangle.

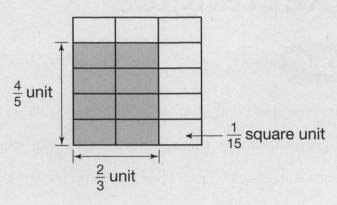

Strategy   Use the properties of the unit square to find the area.

Step 1   Count all parts and the shaded parts.

The unit square is divided into 15 equal parts. There are 8 shaded parts.

Step 2   Add to find the total area.

Each part represents $\frac{1}{15}$ of the unit square.

So, add $\frac{1}{15}$ for each shaded part.

$$\frac{1}{15} + \frac{1}{15} + \frac{1}{15} + \frac{1}{15} + \frac{1}{15} + \frac{1}{15} + \frac{1}{15} + \frac{1}{15} = \frac{8}{15}$$

$\frac{8}{15}$ of the square is shaded.

The area of the rectangle is $\frac{8}{15}$ square unit.

Step 3   Multiply to find the area.

Use the formula for the area of a rectangle.

$A = l \times w$

$\quad = \frac{2}{3} \times \frac{4}{5}$ Use $\frac{2}{3}$ for l and $\frac{4}{5}$ for w.

$\quad = \frac{2 \times 4}{3 \times 5}$ Multiply the numerators and multiply the denominators.

$\quad = \frac{8}{15}$

Solution   The area of the rectangle is $\frac{8}{15}$ square unit.

Example 2

Find the area of the shaded rectangle.

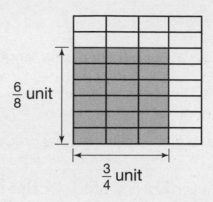

$\frac{6}{8}$ unit

$\frac{3}{4}$ unit

Strategy   **Use the formula for the area of a rectangle.**

Step 1   Multiply the length by the width.

$A = l \times w$

$= \dfrac{3}{4} \times \dfrac{6}{8}$ Substitute $\dfrac{3}{4}$ for l and $\dfrac{6}{8}$ for w.

$= \dfrac{3 \times 6}{4 \times 8}$ Multiply the numerators and multiply the denominators.

$= \dfrac{18}{32} = \dfrac{9}{16}$

Step 2   Check the reasonableness of your answer.

The area of the unit square is 1. More than half of the square is shaded, so the area of the rectangle should be greater than $\dfrac{1}{2}$. Because $\dfrac{9}{16}$ is greater than $\dfrac{1}{2}$, the answer is reasonable.

Solution   **The area of the rectangle is $\dfrac{9}{16}$ square unit.**

Example 3

Draw a model for a rectangle that has a length of $\frac{2}{3}$ unit and a width of $\frac{6}{7}$ unit.
The area of the rectangle is $\frac{12}{21}$ square unit.

Strategy   **Use what you know about fractional side lengths and area.**

> **Step 1**   Draw a unit square. Divide the length of the square into equal parts. Shade the parts that represent the length.
>
> The length has a denominator of 3, so divide the length of the square into 3 equal parts.
>
> The length of each part is $\frac{1}{3}$. Shade 2 of the parts to represent a length of $\frac{2}{3}$ unit.

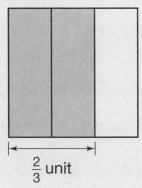

$\frac{2}{3}$ unit

> **Step 2**   Divide the width of the square into equal parts. Shade the parts that represent the width.
>
> The width has a denominator of 7, so divide the width of the square into 7 equal parts.
>
> The width of each part is $\frac{1}{7}$. Shade 6 of the parts to represent a length of $\frac{6}{7}$ unit.

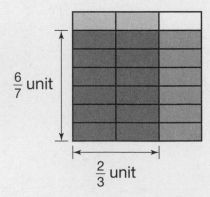

$\frac{6}{7}$ unit

$\frac{2}{3}$ unit

Step 3   Shade the area of the rectangle.

The area of the rectangle is the parts that have been shaded twice.

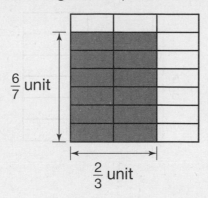

$\frac{6}{7}$ unit

$\frac{2}{3}$ unit

Step 4   Check the model.

The area of the rectangle is $\frac{12}{21}$ square unit. The model has 12 shaded parts out of 21 total parts, so the model is correct.

Solution   The model is shown in Step 3.

Find the area of the rectangle.

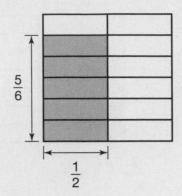

The formula for the area of a rectangle is Area = _____ × _____.

What is the length of the rectangle? _____ unit

What is the width of the rectangle? _____ unit

Find the area. Show your work.

The area of the rectangle is _____ square unit.

Check your answer.

How many parts are shaded in the model? _____

How many total parts are in the model? _____

Write a fraction for the shaded parts. _____

The area of the rectangle is _____ square unit.

1 Look at the diagram below. Use numbers from the box to make the statements true.

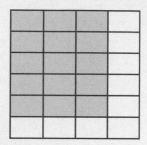

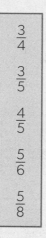

$\frac{3}{4}$

$\frac{3}{5}$

$\frac{4}{5}$

$\frac{5}{6}$

$\frac{5}{8}$

The length of the shaded rectangle is _____ unit.

The width of the shaded rectangle is _____ unit.

The area of the shaded rectangle is _____ square unit.

2 A rectangle has an area of $\frac{12}{36}$ square unit. Which rectangle has the same area? Circle all that apply.

A. length: $\frac{3}{6}$ unit, width: $\frac{4}{6}$ unit

B. length: $\frac{2}{6}$ unit, width: $\frac{6}{8}$ unit

C. length: $\frac{3}{4}$ unit, width: $\frac{4}{9}$ unit

D. length: $\frac{1}{2}$ unit, width: $\frac{12}{18}$ unit

E. length: $\frac{2}{3}$ unit, width: $\frac{6}{12}$ unit

F. length: $\frac{3}{36}$ unit, width: $\frac{4}{36}$ unit

G. length: $\frac{6}{36}$ unit, width: $\frac{6}{36}$ unit

3 A unit square is shown below. Draw and label a model for a rectangle with a length of $\frac{2}{3}$ unit and a width of $\frac{2}{4}$ unit.

What is the area of the rectangle? _____

4 Draw a line from each rectangle to its fractional side lengths.

A.    •   • $\frac{3}{5}$ by $\frac{5}{9}$

B.   •   • $\frac{5}{6}$ by $\frac{2}{3}$

C.   •   • $\frac{3}{4}$ by $\frac{5}{6}$

D.   •   • $\frac{4}{5}$ by $\frac{6}{8}$

5 Two mailing labels are shown. Select True or False for each statement.

Small   Large

$\frac{3}{8}$ in. [rectangle] $\frac{3}{4}$ in. [rectangle]

$\frac{5}{6}$ in. $\frac{5}{6}$ in.

A. The area of the small label is $\frac{5}{16}$ square inch.   ○ True   ○ False

B. The area of the large label is $\frac{5}{12}$ square inch.   ○ True   ○ False

C. The area of the large label is twice the area of the small label.   ○ True   ○ False

D. The sum of the areas of both labels is greater than 1 square unit.   ○ True   ○ False

6 Kira collects stamps. The table shows the lengths and widths of some of her stamps.

Stamp	Length (in inches)	Width (in inches)
A	$\frac{3}{4}$	$\frac{3}{4}$
B	$\frac{5}{6}$	$\frac{1}{2}$
C	$\frac{5}{8}$	$\frac{2}{3}$

Which stamp has the greatest area? Use words, numbers, or models to justify your answer.

7 A mosaic tile is in the shape of a square with side lengths of 1 inch. There is a gray square in the center of the tile.

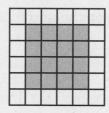

What is the side length of one small shaded square? _____ inch

Is the length of the gray square $\frac{1}{2}$, $\frac{2}{3}$, or $\frac{3}{4}$ the length of the tile? _____

What is the area of the gray square _____ square inch

Does the mosaic tile have more white area or more gray area? Explain your answer.

8 A rectangle has an area of $\frac{15}{100}$ square unit. The length of the rectangle is $\frac{3}{10}$ unit. Find the width of the rectangle.

_____ unit

9 A unit square has been divided into 100 equal parts.

Part A

Find the length, width, and area of the shaded rectangle.

Length: _____ unit

Width: _____ unit

Area: _____ square unit

Part B

Draw and label another rectangle on the grid that has the same area but has a different length and width.

Part C

Show that the rectangles have the same area. Use words, numbers, or models to justify your answer.

Comparing Products to Factors

1 GETTING THE IDEA

Sometimes multiplication can be used for scaling, or resizing. Cody drew a rectangle that is 5 centimeters long. He drew another rectangle that has the same width, but it is 3 times as long.

5 centimeters

5 × 3 centimeters, or 15 centimeters

When you multiply 5 by 3, the product has a value equal to 3 groups of 5. Since this is more than one 5, the product is greater than the factor 5.

When you multiply a given number by a number greater than 1, such as a mixed number, the product is greater than the given number.

Example 1

Multiply $5 \times 2\frac{2}{3}$. How does the product compare to 5?

Strategy   **Use the distributive property.**

Step 1   Use the distributive property to rewrite the problem.

$$5 \times 2\frac{2}{3} = 5 \times \left(2 + \frac{2}{3}\right)$$
$$= (5 \times 2) + \left(5 \times \frac{2}{3}\right)$$

Step 2   Multiply.

$$(5 \times 2) + \left(5 \times \frac{2}{3}\right) = 10 + \left(\frac{5}{1} \times \frac{2}{3}\right)$$
$$= 10 + \frac{10}{3}$$
$$= 10 + 3\frac{1}{3}$$
$$= 13\frac{1}{3}$$

Step 3 ▷ Compare the product to 5.

$$13\tfrac{1}{3} > 5$$

Solution The product, $13\tfrac{1}{3}$, is greater than 5.

When you multiply a given number by a number less than 1, such as a fraction, the product is less than the given number.

Example 2

How does the product of $5 \times \tfrac{3}{4}$ compare to 5? Justify your answer.

Strategy Use reasoning.

Step 1 ▷ Determine what $5 \times \tfrac{3}{4}$ means.

$5 \times \tfrac{3}{4}$ means there are 5 groups of $\tfrac{3}{4}$.

Step 2 ▷ Use reasoning to compare the product of 5 groups of $\tfrac{3}{4}$ to 5.

5 groups of 1 has a product of 5.

Because $\tfrac{3}{4} < 1$, the product of 5 groups of $\tfrac{3}{4}$ will be less than 5.

Solution **The product of 5×1 is 5. Since $\tfrac{3}{4} < 1$, the product of $5 \times \tfrac{3}{4}$ is less than 5.**

You can use similar reasoning to determine what happens when you multiply a fraction by a mixed number or a fraction.

Example 3

How does the product of $\tfrac{3}{4} \times 2\tfrac{2}{3}$ compare to $\tfrac{3}{4}$? Justify your answer.

Strategy Use reasoning.

Step 1 ▷ Compare the factor $2\tfrac{2}{3}$ to 1.

$$2\tfrac{2}{3} > 1$$

Step 2 ▷ Use reasoning to compare the product to $\tfrac{3}{4}$.

$\tfrac{3}{4} \times 1$ has a product of $\tfrac{3}{4}$.

Because $2\tfrac{2}{3} > 1$, the product of $\tfrac{3}{4} \times 2\tfrac{2}{3}$ is greater than $\tfrac{3}{4}$.

Solution **Since $2\tfrac{2}{3} > 1$, the product of $\tfrac{3}{4} \times 2\tfrac{2}{3}$ is greater than $\tfrac{3}{4}$.**

2 COACHED EXAMPLE

How does the product of $\frac{2}{5} \times \frac{3}{4}$ compare to $\frac{2}{5}$ and to $\frac{3}{4}$? Explain your reasoning.

Determine how the product of $\frac{2}{5} \times \frac{3}{4}$ compares to $\frac{2}{5}$.

Compare the factor $\frac{3}{4}$ to 1.

$\frac{3}{4} \bigcirc 1$

$\frac{2}{5} \times 1$ is _____. Since $\frac{3}{4} \bigcirc 1$, the product of $\frac{2}{5} \times \frac{3}{4}$ is _____ than $\frac{2}{5}$.

Determine how the product of $\frac{2}{5} \times \frac{3}{4}$ compares to $\frac{3}{4}$.

Compare the factor $\frac{2}{5}$ to 1.

$\frac{2}{5} \bigcirc 1$

$\frac{3}{4} \times 1$ is _____. Since $\frac{2}{5} \bigcirc 1$, the product of $\frac{2}{5} \times \frac{3}{4}$ is _____ than $\frac{3}{4}$.

The product of $\frac{2}{5} \times \frac{3}{4}$ is _____ **than $\frac{2}{5}$ and** _____ **than $\frac{3}{4}$ because**

_____.

1 Circle the symbol that makes each sentence true.

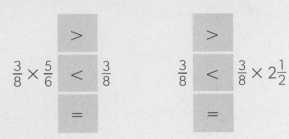

$$\frac{3}{8} \times \frac{5}{6} \quad \boxed{\begin{array}{c} > \\ < \\ = \end{array}} \quad \frac{3}{8} \qquad \frac{3}{8} \quad \boxed{\begin{array}{c} > \\ < \\ = \end{array}} \quad \frac{3}{8} \times 2\frac{1}{2}$$

2 Is the product greater than 7? Select Yes or No. Determine your answers without calculating the products.

A. $7 \times \frac{9}{16}$ ○ Yes   ○ No

B. $7 \times 7\frac{1}{7}$ ○ Yes   ○ No

C. $7 \times 1\frac{7}{10}$ ○ Yes   ○ No

D. $7 \times \frac{7}{7}$ ○ Yes   ○ No

E. $7 \times \frac{21}{7}$ ○ Yes   ○ No

3 Gabriella lives in Oklahoma. The land area of Oklahoma is 68,667 square miles. Gabriella read these facts about the size of other states compared to Oklahoma.

- Arizona is about $1\frac{2}{3}$ the size of Oklahoma.

- Florida is about $\frac{4}{5}$ the size of Oklahoma.

- Vermont is about $\frac{1}{8}$ the size of Oklahoma.

- California is about $2\frac{1}{4}$ the size of Oklahoma.

- Alaska is about $8\frac{1}{3}$ the size of Oklahoma.

Which state has a land area greater than the land area of Oklahoma? Circle all that apply.

A. Arizona

B. Florida

C. Vermont

D. California

E. Alaska

4 Compare the product of each multiplication problem to $\frac{7}{16}$. Do **not** calculate the exact answers. Write the problem in the correct box.

$\frac{7}{16} \times 3\frac{3}{4}$	$\frac{7}{16} \times \frac{3}{7}$	$\frac{7}{16} \times 4$
$1 \times \frac{7}{16}$	$\frac{7}{16} \times \frac{3}{3}$	$2\frac{1}{8} \times \frac{7}{16}$

Less than $\frac{7}{16}$	Equal to $\frac{7}{16}$	Greater than $\frac{7}{16}$

5 During basketball practice, Tamika made 24 free throws. Kara made $1\frac{3}{8}$ times as many free throws as Tamika. Rosie made $\frac{5}{6}$ as many free throws as Tamika. Without calculating, order the names of the girls from least number of free throws made to greatest number of free throws made.

_____   _____   _____

least number of
free throws made

greatest number of
free throws made

6 Tonya correctly graphed points on this number line to represent products.

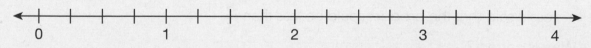

Use the words and numbers from the box to complete the statement.

The point that represents the product of $2\frac{3}{4} \times \frac{3}{4}$ is located to the

_____ of _____ and to the _____

of _____.

left
right
$2\frac{3}{4}$
$\frac{3}{4}$

7 Kenneth built a robot that is $9\frac{1}{4}$ inches tall. He plans to make a scale drawing of the robot. To find the dimensions for the drawing, Kenneth will multiply each dimension of the actual robot by the same factor.

Part A

Describe a factor that Kenneth should use to make a scale drawing that is taller than $9\frac{1}{4}$ inches. Use words, numbers, or models to justify your answer.

Part B

Describe a factor that Kenneth should use to make a scale drawing that is shorter than $9\frac{1}{4}$ inches. Use words, numbers, or models to justify your answer.

8 Lamar and Jessie are multiplying $\frac{7}{12} \times \frac{5}{12}$.

- Lamar said that the product could be less than $\frac{7}{12}$.

- Jessie said that the product could be less than $\frac{5}{12}$.

Who is correct? _____

Explain your reasoning.

9 The table shows the distances Mitch hiked on three days.

Day	Distance Hiked (in miles)
Wednesday	$3\frac{1}{2}$
Thursday	$\frac{5}{8}$
Friday	$3\frac{3}{4}$

On Saturday, Mitch hiked $1\frac{1}{2}$ times as far as he hiked on Friday. How does the distance Mitch hiked on Saturday compare to the distance he hiked on Wednesday? Explain your reasoning.

10 Mrs. Ortega's class is taking a survey of how much sleep fifth graders get.

- Drew said that he usually sleeps for $9\frac{1}{4}$ hours.

- Van reported that he sleeps $1\frac{1}{8}$ times as long as Drew.

- Angie stated that she sleeps $\frac{7}{8}$ as long as Drew.

- Becca said that she sleeps $1\frac{3}{16}$ as long as Drew.

Select True or False for each statement about the length of time the students slept.

A. Angie sleeps longer than Drew. ○ True ○ False

B. Becca sleeps longer than Drew. ○ True ○ False

C. Drew sleeps less than Van. ○ True ○ False

D. Van sleeps longer than Angie. ○ True ○ False

E. Becca sleeps less than Angie. ○ True ○ False

Solving Problems with Multiplying Fractions and Mixed Numbers

1 GETTING THE IDEA -

You can use equations and models to help you solve word problems that involve multiplying fractions and mixed numbers.

Example 1

Deena is tiling a bathroom floor using tiles that are the same size but different colors. So far, she has tiled $\frac{2}{3}$ of the floor. Three-fifths of the tiles she has used are red. What part of the floor is covered with red tiles?

Strategy   **Write an equation, and make a model to represent the problem.**

Step 1   Determine what the problem asks you to find.

You have to find the part of the floor that is covered with red tiles.

Step 2   Identify the information you need to solve the problem.

Deena has covered $\frac{2}{3}$ of the floor with tiles, and $\frac{3}{5}$ of the tiles Deena has used are red.

Step 3   Write an equation.

The word *of* indicates multiplication. So, multiply to find $\frac{3}{5}$ of $\frac{2}{3}$ of the tiles used.

$$\frac{3}{5} \times \frac{2}{3} = \boxed{}$$

Step 4   Solve the problem.

$$\frac{3}{5} \times \frac{2}{3} = \frac{3 \times 2}{5 \times 3}$$
$$= \frac{6}{15} \text{ or } \frac{2}{5}$$

Step 5 Model the problem.

Draw a square to represent the whole floor.

Divide the length of the square into thirds. Shade $\frac{2}{3}$.

Divide the width of the square into fifths. Shade $\frac{3}{5}$.

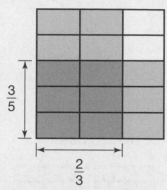

$\frac{6}{15}$ or $\frac{2}{5}$ of the model is shaded twice.

Solution $\frac{2}{5}$ **of the floor is covered with red tiles.**

Example 2

Donovan and Marc weighed their backpacks. Donovan's backpack weighs $5\frac{1}{2}$ pounds. Marc's backpack weighs $\frac{3}{4}$ as much as Donovan's backpack. How much does Marc's backpack weigh?

Strategy **Write an equation, and make a model to represent the problem.**

Step 1 Determine what the problem asks you to find.

You have to find the weight of Marc's backpack.

Step 2 Identify the information you need to solve the problem.

Donovan's backpack weighs $5\frac{1}{2}$ pounds.

Marc's backpack weighs $\frac{3}{4}$ as much as Donovan's backpack.

Step 3 Write an equation.

The words *as much as* indicate multiplication. So, multiply to find $\frac{3}{4}$ as much as $5\frac{1}{2}$ pounds.

$$\frac{3}{4} \times 5\frac{1}{2} = \boxed{}$$

Step 4   Solve the problem.

$$\frac{3}{4} \times 5\frac{1}{2} = \frac{3}{4} \times \frac{11}{2}$$

$$= \frac{3 \times 11}{4 \times 2}$$

$$= \frac{33}{8} \text{ or } 4\frac{1}{8}$$

Step 5   Model the problem.

Draw squares to represent whole pounds.

Shade $5\frac{1}{2}$ of the squares.

Then shade $\frac{3}{4}$ of the shaded parts.

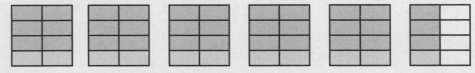

$\frac{33}{8}$ or $4\frac{1}{8}$ of the model is shaded twice.

Solution   Marc's backpack weighs $4\frac{1}{8}$ pounds.

Sometimes it is difficult to make a model of a multiplication word problem. For example, a model of a mixed number multiplied by a mixed number is very complex. However, you can always represent a problem like this with an equation.

Example 3

The movie *Space Storm* is $1\frac{1}{2}$ hours long. *Earth Builders* is $\frac{9}{10}$ as long as *Space Storm*. *Monster Mania* is $1\frac{1}{4}$ as long as *Space Storm*. How long is *Monster Mania*?

Strategy   Write an equation to represent the problem.

Step 1   Determine what the problem asks you to find.

You have to find how many hours long is *Monster Mania*.

Step 2   Identify the information you need to solve the problem.

Monster Mania is $1\frac{1}{4}$ as long as *Space Storm*.

Space Storm is $1\frac{1}{2}$ hours long.

Step 3 Write an equation.

The words *as long as* indicate multiplication. Multiply to find how many hours are $1\frac{1}{4}$ as long as $1\frac{1}{2}$ hours.

$$1\frac{1}{4} \times 1\frac{1}{2} = \boxed{}$$

Step 4 Solve the problem.

$$1\frac{1}{4} \times 1\frac{1}{2} = \frac{5}{4} \times \frac{3}{2}$$
$$= \frac{5 \times 3}{4 \times 2}$$
$$= \frac{15}{8} \text{ or } 1\frac{7}{8}$$

Solution   *Monster Mania* is $1\frac{7}{8}$ hours long.

---

② COACHED EXAMPLE

At Washington Elementary, $\frac{5}{8}$ of the fifth graders are girls. Of the fifth-grade girls, $\frac{1}{4}$ like to play soccer, and $\frac{1}{3}$ like to play basketball. What part of the fifth grade at Washington Elementary are girls who like to play soccer?

The problem asks me to find _____.

The information I need to solve this problem is _____
_____
_____

The operation I can use to solve this problem is _____.

Write an equation. _____

Solve the problem.

Model the problem.

_____ of the fifth grade at Washington Elementary are girls who like to play soccer.

1 Draw a model to represent the problem below.

Jason had $\frac{3}{8}$ of a fence left to paint. He paints $\frac{2}{3}$ of this part of the fence today. What part of the fence does Jason paint today?

2 Mr. Miles uses the recipe shown to make clay for his class.

Modeling Clay

$1\frac{2}{3}$ cups flour

$6\frac{3}{4}$ teaspoons oil

$1\frac{1}{4}$ cups water

$\frac{3}{4}$ cup salt

$4\frac{1}{2}$ teaspoons food coloring

Mix all ingredients. Seal in plastic bag until ready to use.

Select True or False for each statement about the recipe.

A. Use $\frac{5}{6}$ cup flour to make $\frac{1}{2}$ of the recipe.   ○ True   ○ False

B. Use 1 cup salt to make $\frac{3}{4}$ of the recipe.   ○ True   ○ False

C. Use 9 teaspoons oil to make $1\frac{1}{3}$ of the recipe.   ○ True   ○ False

D. Use $8\frac{1}{2}$ teaspoons food coloring to double the recipe.   ○ True   ○ False

3 Which represents the problem shown? Circle all that apply.

Bethany has $1\frac{3}{8}$ yards of orange fabric. She uses $\frac{2}{3}$ of the fabric to make a tote bag. How many yards of fabric does Bethany use for the tote bag?

A.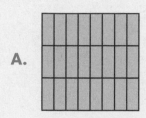

B. $\frac{2}{3} \times 1\frac{3}{8} = \square$

C.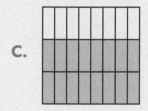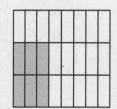

D. $\left(\frac{2}{3} \times 1\right) + \left(\frac{2}{3} \times \frac{3}{8}\right) = \square$

4 The table shows the lengths of some snakes on display at a park's nature center.

Snake	Length (in feet)
Garter Snake	$1\frac{3}{4}$
Green Snake	$1\frac{1}{6}$
Rat Snake	$5\frac{1}{3}$

The center's copperhead is $2\frac{1}{2}$ times the length of its green snake. Its rattlesnake is $\frac{5}{8}$ the length of its rat snake. Its water snake is $1\frac{3}{4}$ times the length of its garter snake. Match the name of each snake to its length.

A. copperhead   •   • $3\frac{1}{16}$ feet

B. rattlesnake   •   • $3\frac{1}{3}$ feet

C. water snake   •   • $2\frac{11}{12}$ feet

5 Use numbers from the box to complete the equation that represents the problem.

A trail mix recipe calls for $\frac{3}{4}$ cup of almonds and $\frac{2}{3}$ cup of coconut. How many cups of almonds are needed to make $\frac{1}{2}$ of the recipe?

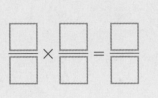 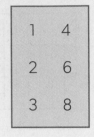

6 Eduardo drew this model to solve a problem.

Fill in the blanks to complete the problem and its solution.

Mike practices the piano each day for _____ hour(s). He uses _____ of this time on finger exercises. For what part of an hour does Mike do finger exercises on the piano each day?

Solution: _____ hour

7 For a party, Jon is making sandwiches that are $1\frac{1}{4}$ feet long. He buys $\frac{7}{8}$ pound of ham and $1\frac{3}{8}$ pounds of turkey for the sandwiches. Then he puts $\frac{1}{6}$ of the meat on each sandwich. How many pounds of meat does Jon put on each sandwich?

_____ pound(s)

8 Ms. Watson is a park planner. She made the two plans shown.

Plan A
Area of park: $7\frac{1}{2}$ acres

Plan B
Area of park: $6\frac{1}{2}$ acres

Part A

How many acres of the park in Plan A are for sports fields?

_____ acre(s)

Part B

How many acres of the park in Plan B are for sports fields?

_____ acre(s)

Part C

Which plan would a person who enjoys playing team sports most likely prefer? Explain your reasoning.

5.NF.7.a, 5.NF.7.b

Dividing Unit Fractions with Whole Numbers

1 GETTING THE IDEA

When you divide a whole number by a unit fraction, you find how many fractional parts are in the whole number.

$6 \div \frac{1}{2} = 12$ Think: There are 12 halves in 6.

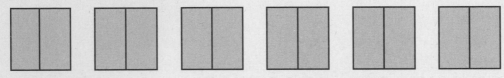

Use the **reciprocal** of the **divisor** to write a multiplication problem.

The reciprocal of $\frac{1}{2}$ is $\frac{2}{1}$.

$$6 \div \frac{1}{2} = 6 \times \frac{2}{1}$$
$$= \frac{6}{1} \times \frac{2}{1}$$
$$= \frac{6 \times 2}{1 \times 1}$$
$$= \frac{12}{1}$$
$$= 12$$

Multiplication and division are **inverse operations**. You can use multiplication to check the **quotient**. Since $6 \div \frac{1}{2} = 12$, then $12 \times \frac{1}{2} = 6$.

Example 1

Divide $3 \div \frac{1}{5}$.

Strategy   Make a model.

Step 1   Model $3 \div \frac{1}{5}$.

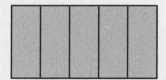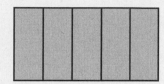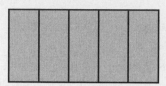

The model shows 3 wholes divided into fifths.
There are 15 fifths in 3 wholes.

Step 2   Use the reciprocal of the divisor to write a multiplication problem. Solve.

The reciprocal of $\frac{1}{5}$ is $\frac{5}{1}$.

$$3 \div \frac{1}{5} = 3 \times \frac{5}{1}$$

$$= \frac{3}{1} \times \frac{5}{1}$$

$$= \frac{3 \times 5}{1 \times 1}$$

$$= \frac{15}{1}$$

$$= 15$$

Step 3   Use multiplication to check.

$$3 \div \frac{1}{5} = 15$$

$$15 \times \frac{1}{5} = \frac{15}{1} \times \frac{1}{5}$$

$$= \frac{15}{5}$$

$$= 3 \checkmark$$

The product is 3. It matches the dividend. So the answer is correct.

Solution $3 \div \frac{1}{5} = 15$

You follow the same procedure when you divide a unit fraction by a whole number.

The reciprocal of a whole number is a **unit fraction**. For example, the reciprocal of 6 is $\frac{1}{6}$.

Example 2

Divide $\frac{1}{5} \div 3$.

Strategy   Use a model.

Step 1   Make a model.

The model shows $\frac{1}{5}$ cut into 3 parts.

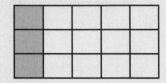

Each part is $\frac{1}{15}$ of the whole.

Step 2   Use the reciprocal of the divisor to write a multiplication problem. Solve.

The reciprocal of 3 is $\frac{1}{3}$.

$$\frac{1}{5} \div 3 = \frac{1}{5} \div \frac{3}{1}$$
$$= \frac{1}{5} \times \frac{1}{3}$$
$$= \frac{1 \times 1}{5 \times 3}$$
$$= \frac{1}{15}$$

Step 3   Use multiplication to check.

$$\frac{1}{5} \div 3 = \frac{1}{15}$$
$$\frac{1}{15} \times 3 = \frac{1}{15} \times \frac{3}{1}$$
$$= \frac{3}{15}$$
$$= \frac{1}{5} \checkmark$$

Solution $\frac{1}{5} \div 3 = \frac{1}{15}$

Example 3

Write a word problem that can be represented by $\frac{1}{2} \div 4 = \boxed{}$. Then solve the problem.

Strategy   **Make a model.**

Step 1   Think about what $\frac{1}{2} \div 4$ means.

$\frac{1}{2} \div 4$ means $\frac{1}{2}$ divided into 4 equal parts.

Step 2   Make a model.

The model shows $\frac{1}{2}$ divided into 4 equal parts.

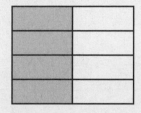

Each part is $\frac{1}{8}$ of the whole.

Step 3   Write a word problem in which $\frac{1}{2}$ of something is divided into 4 equal parts.

Eric has $\frac{1}{2}$ of his library book left to read. He wants to finish the book in 4 days. He decides to read the same amount on each of these days. What part of the book will Eric read each day?

Step 4   Solve the problem.

$$\frac{1}{2} \div 4 = \frac{1}{2} \div \frac{4}{1}$$

$$= \frac{1}{2} \times \frac{1}{4}$$

$$= \frac{1 \times 1}{2 \times 4}$$

$$= \frac{1}{8}$$

Solution   The problem is shown in Step 3. Eric will read $\frac{1}{8}$ of his book each day.

2 COACHED EXAMPLE

Write a word problem that can be represented by $2 \div \frac{1}{3} = \square$. Then solve the problem.

$2 \div \frac{1}{3}$ means dividing __________ into __________.

Make a model to represent $2 \div \frac{1}{3}$.

The model shows that there are __________ thirds in 2.

Write a word problem.

____

____

____

Solve the problem.

The reciprocal of $\frac{1}{3}$ is __________.

Use the reciprocal to write a multiplication problem. Solve.

The solution is ______.

The problem is shown above.

The solution to the problem is ____________________.

1 Lila made a model to solve the equation shown.

$$\frac{1}{4} \div 2 = \boxed{}$$

Draw the model that Lila could have made. Then find the quotient.

$$\frac{1}{4} \div 2 = \underline{}$$

2 Look at each division problem. Is the quotient 12? Select Yes or No.

A. $2 \div \frac{1}{6}$ ○ Yes ○ No

B. $9 \div \frac{1}{3}$ ○ Yes ○ No

C. $\frac{1}{2} \div 6$ ○ Yes ○ No

D. $4 \div \frac{1}{3}$ ○ Yes ○ No

E. $3 \div \frac{1}{4}$ ○ Yes ○ No

3 Find the quotient for each division problem. Compare the quotient to 1. Write the problem in the correct box.

$8 \div \frac{1}{4}$	$16 \div \frac{1}{2}$	$\frac{1}{4} \div 8$	$\frac{1}{3} \div 3$	$\frac{1}{2} \div 16$

Less than 1	Equal to 1	Greater than 1

4 Paulo correctly solved an equation to find how many $\frac{1}{5}$ parts are in 4. Which equation could he have solved? Circle all that apply.

A. $\frac{1}{5} \times 4 = \boxed{}$ E. $4 \div 5 = \boxed{}$

B. $4 \div \frac{1}{5} = \boxed{}$ F. $\boxed{} \times 4 = \frac{1}{5}$

C. $\frac{1}{5} \div 4 = \boxed{}$ G. $4 \times 5 = \boxed{}$

D. $\boxed{} \times \frac{1}{5} = 4$ H. $5 \div 4 = \boxed{}$

5 For each problem in the table, write a problem from the box that has the same value.

Division Problem	Multiplication Problem
$\frac{1}{5} \div 9$	
	5×9
$9 \div \frac{1}{5}$	
	$\frac{1}{9} \times \frac{1}{5}$

$\frac{1}{9} \div 5$

9×5

$\frac{1}{5} \times \frac{1}{9}$

$5 \div 9$

$5 \div \frac{1}{9}$

6 Draw a line from each division equation to the multiplication equation you can use to check the quotient.

A. $3 \div \frac{1}{8} = \boxed{}$ •   • $\frac{1}{24} \times 8 = \boxed{}$

B. $\frac{1}{3} \div 8 = \boxed{}$ •   • $24 \times \frac{1}{3} = \boxed{}$

C. $8 \div \frac{1}{3} = \boxed{}$ •   • $24 \times \frac{1}{8} = \boxed{}$

D. $\frac{1}{8} \div 3 = \boxed{}$ •   • $\frac{1}{24} \times 3 = \boxed{}$

7 Mr. Bond wrote the equation below on the board for his math class to solve.

$$\frac{1}{6} \div 4 = \boxed{}$$

- Luis said that the solution is 24.
- Mateo said that the solution is $\frac{1}{24}$.

Who is correct? Use words, numbers, or models to explain your reasoning.

8 Explain how you can use multiplication to find the quotient of $2 \div \frac{1}{10}$. Then explain how you can use multiplication to check your work.

9 Circle the divisor and factor that make the equations true.

$$\frac{1}{5} \div \begin{array}{c} \frac{1}{8} \\ 8 \\ \frac{8}{8} \end{array} = \frac{1}{40} \qquad \frac{1}{40} \times \begin{array}{c} \frac{1}{8} \\ 8 \\ \frac{8}{8} \end{array} = \frac{1}{5}$$

10 Dante wants to explain division of a unit fraction by a whole number to a classmate.

Part A

Write a word problem that Dante could use to explain when you may need to divide a unit fraction by a whole number.

Part B

Write and solve a division equation that Dante could use to solve the problem.

_____

11 Look at the information about watermelons.

20-Pound Watermelon

6 pounds rind

14 pounds fruit

Use a piece of information about watermelons to write a word problem that can be solved by dividing with a whole number and a unit fraction. Solve the problem you wrote. Show your work. Use a separate piece of paper if necessary.

Solving Problems with Division of Unit Fractions and Whole Numbers

 1 GETTING THE IDEA

Writing an equation can help you solve a word problem. To write a division equation, identify the **dividend** and the divisor. The dividend is the number of objects or the part of an object that is being divided. The divisor is the number of parts or the size of the parts into which you are dividing the dividend.

7 wholes divided into parts that are $\frac{1}{6}$ of a whole equal how many parts?

dividend   divisor
↓   ↓

$$7 \div \frac{1}{6} = \boxed{}$$

$\frac{1}{6}$ divided into 7 parts equals what size parts?

dividend   divisor
↓   ↓

$$\frac{1}{6} \div 7 = \boxed{}$$

Example 1

Bryce made 4 small pies. He cut each into equal-size servings. Each serving is $\frac{1}{2}$ of a pie. How many servings are in the pies Bryce made?

Strategy   **Write an equation, and make a model to represent the problem.**

Step 1   Determine what the problem asks you to find.

You have to find how many servings Bryce made.

Step 2   Identify the information you need to answer the question.

Bryce made 4 pies.

Each serving is $\frac{1}{2}$ of a pie.

Step 3   Make a model to represent the problem.

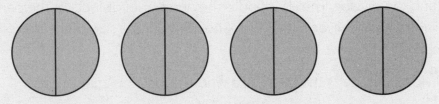

Step 4   Write an equation.

Divide to find how many $\frac{1}{2}$ parts of a pie are in 4 pies.

The dividend is the 4 pies that are cut into servings.

The divisor is the size of each serving, $\frac{1}{2}$ of a pie.

$$4 \div \frac{1}{2} = \boxed{}$$

Step 5   Solve the equation.

$$4 \div \frac{1}{2} = \frac{4}{1} \div \frac{1}{2}$$
$$= \frac{4}{1} \times \frac{2}{1}$$
$$= \frac{4 \times 2}{1 \times 1}$$
$$= \frac{8}{1}$$
$$= 8$$

Step 6   Use inverse operations to check your answer.

If $4 \div \frac{1}{2} = 8$, then $8 \times \frac{1}{2} = 4$.

$$8 \times \frac{1}{2} = \frac{8}{1} \times \frac{1}{2} = \frac{8}{2} = 4 \checkmark$$

Solution   **There are 8 servings in the pies Bryce made.**

Example 2

Shonda has $\frac{1}{2}$ of a large pizza left over. She cuts it into 4 servings that are each the same size. What part of the pizza is each serving?

Strategy   Write an equation, and make a model to represent the problem.

Step 1   Determine what the problem asks you to find.

You have to find the part of the pizza each serving is.

Step 2   Identify the information you need to answer the question.

Shonda has $\frac{1}{2}$ of a pizza.

She cuts it into 4 same-size servings.

Step 3   Make a model.

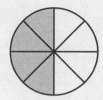

Step 4   Write an equation.

Divide to find the size of each of 4 servings cut from $\frac{1}{2}$ of a pizza.

The dividend is $\frac{1}{2}$ of the pizza that is cut into servings.

The divisor is the 4 servings that are cut.

$\frac{1}{2} \div 4 = \boxed{}$

Step 5   Solve the equation.

$$\frac{1}{2} \div 4 = \frac{1}{2} \div \frac{4}{1}$$
$$= \frac{1}{2} \times \frac{1}{4}$$
$$= \frac{1 \times 1}{2 \times 4}$$
$$= \frac{1}{8}$$

Step 6   Use inverse operations to check your answer.

If $\frac{1}{2} \div 4 = \frac{1}{8}$, then $\frac{1}{8} \times 4 = \frac{1}{2}$.

$\frac{1}{8} \times 4 = \frac{1}{8} \times \frac{4}{1} = \frac{4}{8} = \frac{1}{2}$ ✓

Solution   Each serving is $\frac{1}{8}$ of the pizza.

Three acres of a park are used for a community garden. The garden is divided into plots. Each person who wants a garden gets one plot. Each plot is $\frac{1}{8}$ acre. How many garden plots are in the park?

You have to find _____.

The information you need to solve the problem is _____

_____

_____

Make a model to represent the problem.

Write an equation. _____ ÷ _____ = ☐

The dividend is the number of _____.

The divisor is the size of each _____.

Solve the equation.

Use inverse operations to check your answer.

There are _____ garden plots in the park.

1 Which represents the problem shown? Check all that apply.

Kara read 6 pages of a book in $\frac{1}{3}$ hour. It took her the same length of time to read each page. How long did it take Kara to read each page?

A.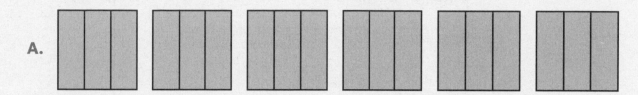

B.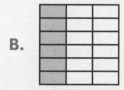

C. $\frac{1}{3} \div 6 = \boxed{}$

D. $6 \div \frac{1}{3} = \boxed{}$

2 A recipe for 3 dozen rolls calls for $\frac{1}{3}$ cup of shortening. How much shortening is needed to make 1 dozen rolls?

3 A store sells $\frac{1}{4}$ pound of cashews for $2.

- Julio used $\frac{1}{4} \div 2 = \boxed{}$ to find how many pounds of cashews he can buy for $1.

- Dana used $2 \div \frac{1}{4} = \boxed{}$ to find how many pounds of cashews she can buy for $1.

Who is correct? Explain your answer.

4 The graph shows the length of some fish that Steven caught one summer.

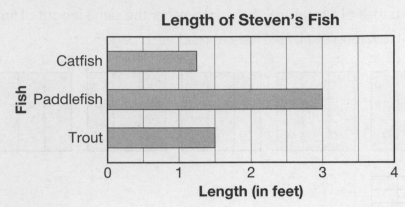

Length of Steven's Fish

Steven often uses minnows as bait when fishing. A minnow is about $\frac{1}{4}$ foot long. About how many times longer is a paddlefish than a minnow?

_____ times

5 The amount of cereal that makes one serving is different for different brands. Mr. Madison wants to buy a box of cereal that has 7 or more servings. Sort the boxes of cereal according to the number of servings. Write each brand in the correct box.

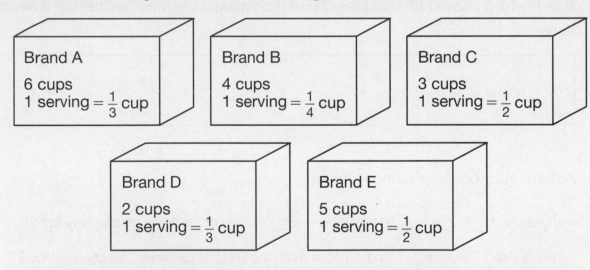

Brand A
6 cups
1 serving = $\frac{1}{3}$ cup

Brand B
4 cups
1 serving = $\frac{1}{4}$ cup

Brand C
3 cups
1 serving = $\frac{1}{2}$ cup

Brand D
2 cups
1 serving = $\frac{1}{3}$ cup

Brand E
5 cups
1 serving = $\frac{1}{2}$ cup

Less than 7 Servings	7 or More Servings

6 Tina drew this model to solve a problem.

Fill in the blanks to complete the problem and its solution.

Brookside School is having a talent show. The show will last for _____ hour(s). Each student may perform for _____ of an hour. How many students may perform during the show?

_____ students

7 Select True or False for each statement about the problem shown.

Miles bought a 7-pound bag of food for his puppy. There are 35 cups of food in the bag. Miles feeds his puppy $\frac{1}{3}$ cup of food twice a day. How many servings of puppy food will Miles get from the bag of food?

A. To solve this problem, you can use 7 as the dividend.	○ True	○ False
B. To solve this problem, you can use $\frac{1}{3}$ as the divisor.	○ True	○ False
C. To solve this problem, you can use 7 as the divisor.	○ True	○ False
D. To solve this problem, you can use 35 as the dividend.	○ True	○ False
E. You can use the equation $35 \div \frac{1}{3}$ to solve this problem.	○ True	○ False
F. You can use the equation $\frac{1}{3} \div 35$ to solve this problem.	○ True	○ False
G. Miles will get 35 servings of puppy food from the bag.	○ True	○ False

8 Maddie correctly solved the problem shown. Select a step Maddie could have taken. Circle all that apply.

For a party, Elias makes $2\frac{1}{2}$ cups of chicken salad and $3\frac{1}{2}$ cups of egg salad. He puts $\frac{1}{4}$ cup of salad on each sandwich he makes. Some sandwiches are made with both chicken and egg salad. How many sandwiches can Elias make?

A. Add $2\frac{1}{2}$ and $3\frac{1}{2}$.

B. Divide $\frac{1}{4}$ by the sum of $2\frac{1}{2}$ and $3\frac{1}{2}$.

C. Divide the sum of $2\frac{1}{2}$ and $3\frac{1}{2}$ by $\frac{1}{4}$.

D. Multiply the sum of $2\frac{1}{2}$ and $3\frac{1}{2}$ by $\frac{1}{4}$.

E. Subtract $\frac{1}{4}$ from the sum of $2\frac{1}{2}$ and $3\frac{1}{2}$.

9 Megan is making a quilt. She bought $\frac{1}{3}$ yard of fabric to use for the border of the quilt.

Part A

Megan cut the fabric into 4 same-size strips. What part of a yard is each strip?

_____ yard

Part B

Megan used only 3 of the strips to make the border. How much fabric did she use for the border?

_____ yard

10 The students in an art class are making beaded necklaces.

• Bella made a necklace 16 inches long with beads that are $\frac{1}{8}$ inch in diameter.

• Edgar used $\frac{1}{2}$-inch-wide beads to make a 22-inch necklace.

• Marla used beads that are $\frac{1}{4}$ inch in diameter to make a necklace 18 inches long.

Write the names of the students in order. Start with the student who used the least number of beads. End with the student who used the greatest number of beads.

_____ _____ _____
  least number   greatest number
   of beads   of beads

1 A park is in the shape of a rectangle. The park is $\frac{5}{8}$ mile long and $\frac{2}{3}$ mile wide. What is the area of the park? Use a model if necessary.

2 Select True or False for each equation.

    A. $\frac{7}{15} + \frac{1}{3} = \frac{4}{5}$ ○ True   ○ False

    B. $2\frac{3}{4} - \frac{1}{2} = 1\frac{1}{4}$ ○ True   ○ False

    C. $\frac{6}{7} - \frac{2}{5} = \frac{3}{35}$ ○ True   ○ False

    D. $1\frac{2}{9} + 2\frac{1}{4} = 3\frac{17}{36}$ ○ True   ○ False

3 Marcus volunteered for $4\frac{1}{2}$ hours this week. Beth volunteered for $1\frac{1}{2}$ times as long as Marcus. For how many hours did Beth volunteer? Use words, numbers, or a model to justify your answer.

4 Circle the divisor and factor that make the equations true.

$$\frac{1}{4} \div \begin{array}{c} \frac{1}{6} \\ 6 \\ \frac{6}{6} \end{array} = \frac{1}{24} \qquad \frac{1}{24} \times \begin{array}{c} \frac{1}{6} \\ 6 \\ \frac{6}{6} \end{array} = \frac{1}{4}$$

5 Drew hiked two trails at a state park. Rocky Hill Trail is $\frac{7}{8}$ mile long. Babbling Brook Trail is $\frac{4}{5}$ mile long. How much farther did Drew hike on the Rocky Hill Trail than on the Babbling Brook Trail?

Write an equation to represent the situation using a common denominator.

_____

Drew hiked _____ mile farther on the Rocky Hill Trail.

6 Find each product. Compare the product to 1. Write the multiplication problem in the correct box.

| $\frac{2}{5} \times 2$ | $\frac{4}{3} \times 6$ | $\frac{10}{6} \times \frac{6}{10}$ | $\frac{2}{9} \times \frac{5}{7}$ | $\frac{8}{7} \times \frac{1}{2}$ | $8 \times \frac{4}{5}$ |

Less than 1	Equal to 1	Greater than 1

7 Nina used $3\frac{1}{2}$ pounds of apples to make applesauce. She used $\frac{3}{4}$ times as many apples to make apple pies. How does the number of pounds of apples Nina used for apple pies compare to the amount she used for applesauce? Explain your reasoning.

8 Select True or False for each statement about the problem below.

Mr. Graham buys clay for the art class in 25-pound blocks. He gave out a total of 15 pounds of clay to a class of students for a project. Each student got $\frac{1}{2}$ pound of clay. How many students are in the class?

A. You can use the equation $\frac{1}{2} \div 15$ to solve this problem.　○ True　○ False

B. You can use the equation $15 \div \frac{1}{2}$ to solve this problem.　○ True　○ False

C. To solve this problem, you can use 15 as the dividend.　○ True　○ False

D. To solve this problem, you can use $\frac{1}{2}$ as the divisor.　○ True　○ False

E. To solve this problem, you can use 25 as the dividend.　○ True　○ False

F. There are 30 students in the class.　○ True　○ False

9 Draw a line from each rectangle to the equation that represents the area of the rectangle.

A.　• 　　　•　$\frac{1}{2} \times \frac{3}{5} = \frac{3}{10}$

B.　• 　　　•　$\frac{3}{4} \times \frac{2}{5} = \frac{3}{10}$

C.　• 　　　•　$\frac{2}{5} \times \frac{2}{3} = \frac{4}{15}$

D.　• 　　　•　$\frac{3}{4} \times \frac{1}{2} = \frac{3}{8}$

10 Which represents the problem shown? Circle all that apply.

Every Saturday, Greg walks $2\frac{1}{4}$ miles to the park to play basketball with friends. He walks $\frac{2}{3}$ of this distance when he walks to school. How far does Greg walk to school?

A. $\frac{2}{3} + 2\frac{1}{4} = \boxed{}$

B.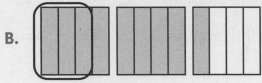

C. $\frac{2}{3} \times 2\frac{1}{4} = \boxed{}$

D.

E. $2\frac{1}{4} \times \frac{2}{3} = \boxed{}$

11 For each problem in the table, write a problem from the box that has the same value. Use problems from the box.

Division Problem	Multiplication Problem
$8 \div \frac{1}{15}$	
	$\frac{1}{15} \times \frac{1}{8}$
$\frac{1}{8} \div 15$	
	15×8

$\frac{1}{8} \times \frac{1}{15}$

$\frac{1}{15} \div 8$

8×15

$15 \div \frac{1}{8}$

12 Jake's ride home from band camp takes $4\frac{1}{2}$ hours. Lela's ride home is $1\frac{1}{3}$ times as long as Jake's ride home. Amy's ride home is $\frac{3}{4}$ as long as Jake's ride home. Without calculating, order the names of the bandmates from the longest ride home to the shortest ride home.

_____ _____ _____

longest ride home   shortest ride home

13 Five friends picked 7 pounds of apples. They will share the apples equally.

Part A

Draw a model to show how much each friend will receive.

Part B

Write and solve an equation to represent the problem. How much does each friend receive?

_____

14 Find two fractions from the box that can be added using the denominator 18. Write those two fractions, and then find the sum.

_____ + _____ = _____

$\frac{5}{8}$	$\frac{4}{7}$
$\frac{3}{4}$	$\frac{5}{12}$
$\frac{7}{9}$	$\frac{1}{6}$

15 Kyle has $\frac{2}{3}$ of a carton of eggs. He uses $\frac{1}{2}$ of the eggs that are left.

Draw a model to represent the problem. Write and solve an equation for the model.

Painting a Mural

You are the president of the Marine Biology Club. There are 24 students in the club who are painting a mural of the sea. The mural will cover most of one wall in the classroom.

- Each student will paint one rectangular part of the mural.
- Each part will be the same size and shape.
- In each part, a student will paint one of the following types of sea life: coral, fish, or dolphins.

Part A The rectangular wall is shown at right. Draw one way the mural could be divided into parts for the students to paint. Label the length, width, and area of one part. Explain how you found these measurements.

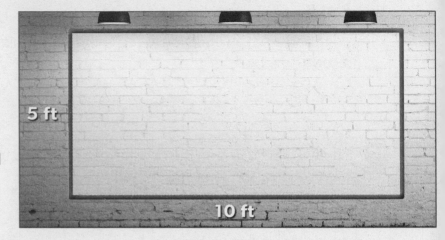

Part B Alex says that the mural could have been divided into rectangles that are each $\frac{1}{2}$ foot wide. Is Alex correct? Explain your answer.

Part C On Monday, some of the students painted their parts of the mural. Complete the table to show the fraction of the mural that is painted with each type of sea life.

Parts of the Mural Painted on Monday

Sea Life	Number of Students	Fraction of Mural
Coral	2	
Fish	8	
Dolphins	4	

What fraction of the mural still needs to be painted? Show your work.

Part D Your teacher would like for the mural to be completed by the end of the day on Tuesday. Create a plan for how many of the remaining students you will assign to paint each type of sea life on Tuesday to complete the mural. Use fractions to verify that your plan will work.

Part E On Tuesday morning, your teacher tells you that each type of sea life must cover equal parts of the mural. This means that there should be the same number of parts with dolphins, with fish, and with coral. Will you need to change your plan from Part D so that each type of sea life covers an equal area of the mural? If so, how will you change it? Explain your answer.

DOMAIN 4

Measurement and Data

Converting Measurement Units

When you **convert** measurement units, you change the unit to a larger or smaller unit.

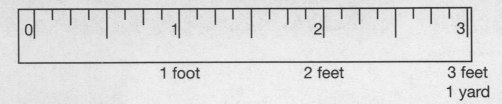

1 foot   2 feet   3 feet
                                1 yard

1 yard = 3 feet

- Multiply to convert to a smaller unit of measurement.

  Convert 8 yards to feet. 8 yards × 3 feet = 24 feet

- Divide to convert to a larger unit of measurement.

  Convert 9 feet to yards. 9 feet ÷ 3 feet = 3 yards

Example 1

How many seconds are in 5 hours?

Strategy   **Use time equivalents to compare the size of the units.**

Step 1   Write time equivalents for seconds, minutes, and hours.

   1 hour = 60 minutes

   1 minute = 60 seconds

Step 2   Decide if you will multiply or divide.

   An hour is a larger unit than a minute, and a minute is a larger unit than a second. To convert to a smaller unit, multiply.

Step 3   Multiply to convert hours to minutes.

   5 hours × 60 minutes = 300 minutes

Step 4   Multiply to convert minutes to seconds.

   300 minutes × 60 seconds = 18,000 seconds

Solution   **There are 18,000 seconds in 5 hours.**

Example 2

Malia wants to sew a border 2 meters long for a quilt. She has 3 pieces of purple ribbon, each 70 centimeters long. Does she have enough ribbon for the border?

Strategy   **Compare the total length of the pieces of ribbon with 2 meters.**

Step 1   Find the total length of ribbon Malia has.

She has 3 pieces, each 70 centimeters long.

3×70 centimeters $= 210$ centimeters

Step 2   Decide if you will multiply or divide.

To convert 210 centimeters (smaller unit) to meters (larger unit), you need to divide.

Step 3   Convert centimeters to meters.

100 centimeters $= 1$ meter

210 centimeters $\div$ 100 centimeters $= 2.10$ meters

Step 4   Compare the two measurements.

Malia needs 2 meters for the border.

2.10 meters > 2 meters

Solution   **Malia has enough ribbon for the border.**

Example 3

A restaurant has 2 gallons of vegetable soup and 5 quarts of chicken noodle soup. How many 2-cup servings of each kind of soup can be served? How many total servings of soup?

Strategy   **Convert gallons and quarts to cups.**

Step 1   Convert gallons (larger unit) to cups (smaller unit).

There are 2 gallons of vegetable soup.

1 gallon $= 4$ quarts $= 8$ pints $= 16$ cups

2 gallons $= 2 \times 16 = 32$ cups

There are 32 cups of vegetable soup.

Step 2   Find the number of servings of vegetable soup.

A serving is 2 cups.

32 cups $\div$ 2 cups $= 16$ servings of vegetable soup

Step 3	Convert quarts (larger unit) to cups (smaller unit).

There are 5 quarts of chicken noodle soup.

1 quart = 2 pints = 4 cups

5 quarts = 5 × 4 = 20 cups

There are 20 cups of chicken noodle soup.

Step 4	Find the number of servings of chicken noodle soup.

A serving is 2 cups.

20 cups ÷ 2 cups = 10 servings

Step 5	Find the total number of servings of soup.

16 servings + 10 servings = 26 total servings

Solution There are 16 servings of vegetable soup and 10 servings of chicken noodle soup. So, there are 26 total servings of soup.

Example 4

Mrs. Diaz bought a pumpkin with a mass of 4,700 grams. She used 2.5 kilograms of pulp for a pumpkin pie and roasted 0.3 kilogram of seeds for a snack. What is the remaining mass of the pumpkin?

Strategy Convert the mass of the whole pumpkin to kilograms.

Step 1	Convert 4,700 grams (smaller unit) to kilograms (larger unit).

Divide.

1,000 grams = 1 kilogram

4,700 ÷ 1,000 = 4.700 or 4.7 kilograms

Step 2	Find the total mass of pulp and seeds.

2.5 kilograms + 0.3 kilogram = 2.8 kilograms

Step 3	Subtract to find the part remaining.

4.7 kilograms − 2.8 kilograms = 1.9 kilograms

Solution The remaining mass of the pumpkin after the seeds and pulp are removed is 1.9 kilograms.

Nikki and Manuel picked 75 pounds of apples. If each apple weighs about 5 ounces, how many apples did they pick?

You need to convert _____ to _____.

To convert from a _____ unit to a _____ unit, you need to _____.

   1 pound = _____ ounces

Convert.

   _____ ◯ _____ = _____

To find the number of apples, divide _____ by _____.

Solve to find the number of apples.

   _____ ◯ _____ = _____

Nikki and Manual picked _____ apples.

1 Draw a line from each measure to its equivalent measure.

A. 3 meters   •   • 3 centimeters

B. 30 kilometers •   • 300 centimeters

C. 30 centimeters •   • 0.3 meters

D. 30 millimeters •   • 30,000 meters

2 Are the measures equivalent? Select Yes or No.

A. 4 pounds = 64 ounces   ○ Yes ○ No

B. 200 centimeters = 2 meters   ○ Yes ○ No

C. 2 kilograms = 200 grams   ○ Yes ○ No

D. 4 liters = 4,000 milliliters ○ Yes ○ No

E. 2 tons = 200 pounds   ○ Yes ○ No

3 Circle the numbers to make equivalent measures.

5		0.005	
50	milliliters =	0.05	liters
500		5	

4 Select a true statement about converting units of measurement. Circle all that apply.

A. Divide to convert gallons to cups.

B. Multiply to convert pounds to ounces.

C. Divide to convert meters to kilometers.

D. Multiply to convert grams to kilograms.

E. Multiply to convert hours to seconds.

F. Divide to convert milliliters to liters.

5 Jake runs either 15 kilometers or 8,500 meters each day. He alternates short and long runs. How many meters farther will he run on his two long run days than on his two short run days? Describe how you found your answer.

[blank answer box]

6 Compare each measurement to 2 quarts. Write the measurements in the correct box.

| $\frac{1}{2}$ gallon | 6 cups | 1 gallon | 4 pints | 8 cups | 6 pints |

Less than 2 Quarts	Equal to 2 Quarts	More than 2 Quarts

7 Mrs. Johnson has 2 kilograms of apples, 0.5 kilogram of pears, and 1,500 grams of bananas. She chops the fruit into small pieces and mixes them together. Then she divides the mixture equally into 4 bowls.

| 500 |
| 1,000 |
| 1,500 |
| 2,000 |
| 4,000 |
| 5,000 |

Use the numbers from the box to complete the sentences.

There are _____ gram(s) of apples and _____ gram(s) of pears.

The finished fruit mixture has a mass of _____ gram(s), so each

bowl holds _____ gram(s) of fruit.

8 Omar is excited about going on a camping trip with his friends. The trip is in 8 days. He is counting down the hours and minutes until the trip. Select the numbers from each column to make the statement true.

96	11,520

The camping trip will occur in

192

hours or

4,608

minutes.

240	2,880

9 A stock clerk is arranging a case of 24 bottles of shampoo on a shelf. Each bottle contains 375 mL of shampoo. How many liters of shampoo do all the bottles contain? Show your work.

10 Find the area in square yards of Kev's field of winter squash. Remember to first convert feet to yards.

96 ft

345 ft

Area = _____ square yards

11 Emma's plant grew $\frac{1}{2}$ inch in one day. Suppose the plant continues to grow at the same rate. How tall will it be in 5 weeks? Justify your answer.

12 Duane carries all of these books in his backpack.

Book	Weight
Mathematics	$3\frac{3}{4}$ lb.
Science	55 oz.
Social Studies	$2\frac{1}{4}$ lb.
Literature 1	11 oz.
Literature 2	14 oz.

Part A

What is the total weight in pounds of the books in Duane's backpack?

Part B

What is the total weight in ounces of the books in Duane's backpack?

Part C

Tonight, Duane needs to bring home only his math and science textbooks. Tomorrow, he has to bring his science project to school. His project weighs 5 pounds. Find the total weight Duane will carry in his backpack tomorrow.

Line Plots with Fractions

1 GETTING THE IDEA

You can use a **line plot** to study and interpret data. A line plot organizes data on a number line. Each piece of data is shown by an "X" above the number line. The Xs show the **frequency**, or the number of times something occurs.

This line plot shows measurement data. Students in a science class collected small objects and measured them to the nearest $\frac{1}{8}$ inch.

Length of Found Object (nearest $\frac{1}{8}$ inch)

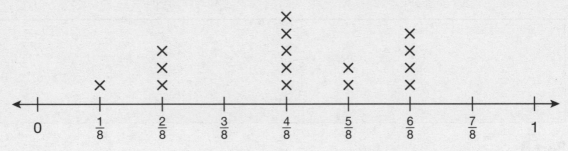

Each X represents one measurement. There are 15 Xs, so 15 objects were found and measured.

There are 5 Xs above $\frac{4}{8}$, so 5 small objects measured about $\frac{4}{8}$ or $\frac{1}{2}$ inch.

Example 1

A group of students measured the length of some used crayons. This list shows the measurements for different crayon colors to the nearest $\frac{1}{2}$ inch. Make a line plot of the data.

Fire Red: 1 inch   Pine Green: $1\frac{1}{2}$ inches

Sky Blue: $1\frac{1}{2}$ inches   Mahogany: 2 inches

Blush: $2\frac{1}{2}$ inches   Plum: $1\frac{1}{2}$ inches

Eggplant: $1\frac{1}{2}$ inches   Lemon Yellow: 1 inch

Pumpkin: $2\frac{1}{2}$ inches   Mist Gray: 3 inches

Strategy   Draw and label a number line. Then mark the frequency of each measurement with Xs.

Step 1   Record the frequency of each measurement.

Make a frequency chart to organize the data.

Crayon length (in inches)	1	$1\frac{1}{2}$	2	$2\frac{1}{2}$	3
Frequency	2	4	1	2	1

Step 2   Draw and label a number line with $\frac{1}{2}$-inch intervals. Include a title.

The measurements range from 1 inch to 3 inches with $\frac{1}{2}$-inch intervals.

Label the number line with the numbers 1, $1\frac{1}{2}$, 2, $2\frac{1}{2}$, and 3.

Length of Crayons (nearest $\frac{1}{2}$ inch)

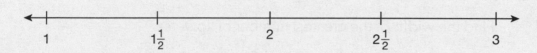

Step 3   Mark Xs above each measurement on the number line.

Two crayons measured 1 inch, so make 2 Xs above the label 1. Four crayons measured $1\frac{1}{2}$ inches, so make 4 Xs above the label $1\frac{1}{2}$, and so on.

Length of Crayons (nearest $\frac{1}{2}$ inch)

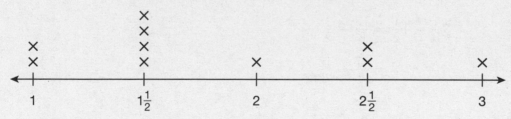

Solution   A line plot of the data is shown in Step 3.

Example 2

The line plot shows the widths of several different flowers measured to the nearest $\frac{1}{8}$ inch. What is the difference between the width of the greatest number of flowers and the width of the least number of flowers?

Width of Flower (nearest $\frac{1}{8}$ inch)

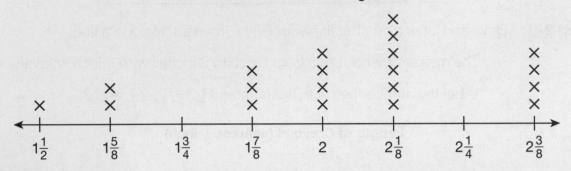

Strategy Analyze the data to find the greatest and least frequencies.

Step 1 Find the width of the greatest number of flowers.

The most Xs are above $2\frac{1}{8}$, so $2\frac{1}{8}$ inches has the greatest frequency.

There are 6 flowers that measured $2\frac{1}{8}$ inches in width.

Step 2 Find the width of the least number of flowers.

There is only 1 X above $1\frac{1}{2}$, so $1\frac{1}{2}$ inches has the least frequency.

Step 3 Subtract to find the difference.

$$2\frac{1}{8} - 1\frac{1}{2} = \frac{17}{8} - \frac{3}{2}$$

$$= \frac{17}{8} - \frac{12}{8}$$

$$= \frac{5}{8}$$

Solution The difference is $\frac{5}{8}$ inch.

Example 3

The line plot shows the amount of juice that students left in their cups after breakfast. What is the amount of juice in each cup if all of the leftover juice was distributed equally?

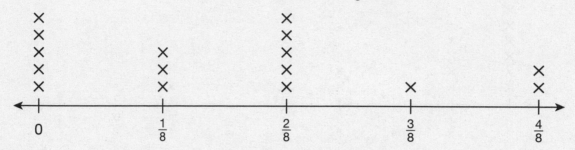

Leftover Juice (nearest $\frac{1}{8}$ cup)

Strategy Use division to distribute the leftover juice equally.

Step 1 Find the total amount of leftover juice.

Multiply each measurement by the number of Xs above it.

5 Xs above 0: $5 \times 0 = 0$ Five students drank all their juice, so nothing was left in their cups.

3 Xs above $\frac{1}{8}$: $3 \times \frac{1}{8} = \frac{3}{8}$

5 Xs above $\frac{2}{8}$: $5 \times \frac{2}{8} = \frac{10}{8}$

1 X above $\frac{3}{8}$: $1 \times \frac{3}{8} = \frac{3}{8}$

2 Xs above $\frac{4}{8}$: $2 \times \frac{4}{8} = \frac{8}{8}$

Add. $0 + \frac{3}{8} + \frac{10}{8} + \frac{3}{8} + \frac{8}{8} = \frac{24}{8} = 3$

Step 2 Find the number of juice cups.

Each X represents a cup with the amount of juice left by one student.

Add the number of Xs above each number on the line plot.

$5 + 3 + 5 + 1 + 2 = 16$

There were 16 juice cups.

Step 3 Divide the total amount of juice by the number of juice cups to distribute the juice equally.

$3 \div 16 = \frac{3}{16}$

Solution If the leftover juice were distributed equally, there would be $\frac{3}{16}$ cup of juice left in each cup.

Farah measured the number of inches of rain every day for 2 weeks. The line plot shows her data. What would the total rainfall be if it rains the same amount every 2 weeks for a year?

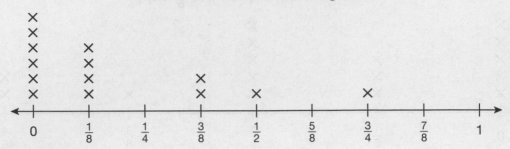

Rainfall Amount (to nearest $\frac{1}{8}$ inch)

First, find the total _____.

It rained 0 inches on _____ days. 0 × _____ = _____

It rained $\frac{1}{8}$ inch on _____ days. _____ × $\frac{1}{8}$ = _____

It rained $\frac{3}{8}$ inch on _____ days. _____ × $\frac{3}{8}$ = _____

It rained _____ inch on 1 day. 1 × _____ = _____

It rained _____ inch on 1 day. 1 × _____ = _____

Next, add the products.

_____ + _____ + _____ + _____ + _____ =

Write equivalent fractions with like denominators.

_____ + _____ + _____ + _____ + _____ = _____

Change the improper fraction to a mixed number.

_____ = _____ = _____

How many 2-week intervals are in 1 year?

1 year = _____ weeks, so divide by 2.

_____ ÷ 2 = _____

Finally, multiply to find the yearly rainfall.

_____ × _____ = _____ × _____ = _____

Change the improper fraction to a whole number.

_____ = _____

If it rains the same amount every 2 weeks for a year, the yearly rainfall will be

_____ inches.

Students measured the length of their pencils to the nearest $\frac{1}{2}$ inch. The line plot shows the data. Use the line plot for problems 1 and 2.

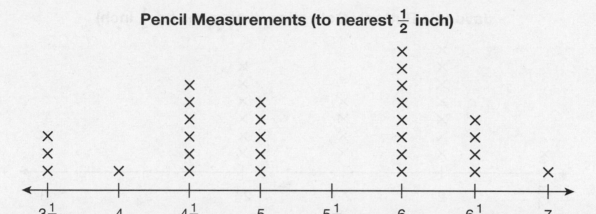

Pencil Measurements (to nearest $\frac{1}{2}$ inch)

1 Choose a number from the box to make the statement true.

$6\frac{1}{2}$
5
$4\frac{1}{2}$
$3\frac{1}{2}$
2

The difference between the length of the longest pencil and the shortest pencil was _____ inches.

2 If the pencils that measured $3\frac{1}{2}$ inches and the pencils that measured $4\frac{1}{2}$ inches were placed end to end, how long would they be? Show your work.

_____ inches

3 Jayden has a collection of butterflies. The line plot shows the wingspan of his butterflies. Select True or False for each statement.

Jayden's Butterfly Collection Wingspans (to $\frac{1}{4}$ inch)

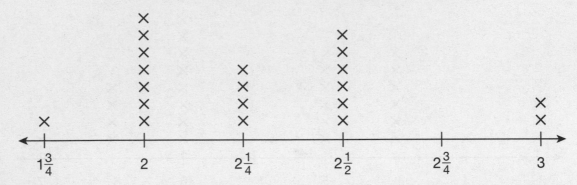

A. The length of the wingspan with the greatest number of Jayden's butterflies is 2 inches.   ○ True   ○ False

B. There are 3 butterflies with a wingspan of 3 inches.   ○ True   ○ False

C. There are 20 butterflies in Jayden's collection.   ○ True   ○ False

D. Half of Jayden's butterflies have a wingspan less than $2\frac{1}{2}$ inches.   ○ True   ○ False

4 Ms. Martinez showed her class a button. Students guessed how wide the button is to the nearest $\frac{1}{8}$ inch. Display the following data on a line plot.

Guesses	$\frac{5}{8}$	$\frac{1}{2}$	$\frac{3}{8}$	$\frac{3}{8}$	$\frac{3}{8}$	$\frac{5}{8}$	$\frac{1}{2}$	$\frac{3}{4}$
	$\frac{1}{2}$	$\frac{3}{8}$	$\frac{3}{8}$	$\frac{1}{2}$	$\frac{5}{8}$	$\frac{1}{2}$	$\frac{3}{8}$	$\frac{3}{8}$

The line plot shows the number of hours Yasumi practiced piano in a week.
Use this line plot for problems 5 and 6.

Yasumi's Piano Practice (in hours)

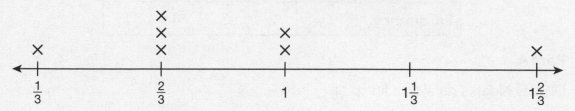

5 Use the numbers in the box to complete the statements.

The greatest amount of time Yasumi practiced in a single

day was _____ hours.

Yasumi practiced for _____ hour(s) the greatest number of times.

Yasumi practiced a total of _____ hours in a week.

$$\frac{2}{3}$$

$$1\frac{1}{3}$$

$$1\frac{2}{3}$$

3

5

6

6 How much time would Yasumi have practiced each day if her total practice time
were divided evenly among the days she practiced? Circle the number to
complete the statement.

$$\frac{2}{3}$$

$$\frac{6}{7}$$

Yasumi would have practiced $\frac{5}{6}$ hour(s) per day.

$$\frac{5}{7}$$

$$\frac{7}{6}$$

7 Noah recorded the weight of tomatoes he picked from his garden on one day.

Weight (in pounds)	$\frac{3}{8}$	$\frac{1}{2}$	$\frac{5}{8}$	$\frac{3}{4}$
Frequency	2	3	4	1

Part A

Display Noah's data on a line plot.

Part B

Noah will package tomatoes. Use the numbers in the box to make the statements true.

To make a package that weighs $1\frac{1}{2}$ pounds, Noah can put

2 tomatoes that weigh _____ pound each with

_____ tomato(es) that weigh(s) _____ pound each.

There will be _____ tomatoes left with a total weight

of _____ pounds.

$\frac{3}{8}$

$\frac{5}{8}$

$\frac{3}{4}$

1

2

$2\frac{1}{2}$

4

7

Understanding Volume

Volume is the measure of the amount of space in a solid figure. It can be measured using a **unit cube**, which is a cube that has a side length of 1 unit and a volume of 1 **cubic unit**.

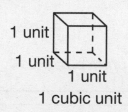

1 unit
1 unit
1 unit
1 cubic unit

Volume can be measured in cubic centimeters, cubic inches, cubic feet, and other cubic units. A **cubic centimeter** is a unit cube with a side length of 1 centimeter. A **cubic inch** is a unit cube with a side length of 1 inch. A **cubic foot** is a unit cube with a side length of 1 foot.

Example 1

Ed used unit cubes to build a solid figure with no gaps or overlaps. He used the unit cube shown. What is the volume of the unit cube?

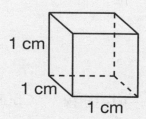

1 cm
1 cm
1 cm

Strategy   Use the definition of a unit cube.

Step 1   Check that each side length is 1 unit.

A unit cube has a side length of 1.

Each side length of this unit cube is 1 centimeter.
The cube is a unit cube.

Step 2   Find the volume of the unit cube.

Read the measurement unit on the cube.

The measurement unit is centimeters, so the volume is 1 cubic centimeter.

Solution   **The volume of the unit cube is 1 cubic centimeter.**

A **rectangular prism**, shown below, is a solid figure that has six **faces** that are rectangles. A face of a solid figure is any flat surface of the figure that is a polygon. So, the faces of a cube are all squares, and the faces of a rectangular prism are all rectangles.

The volume of a solid figure can be measured by finding the number of cubic units needed to fill the solid figure without gaps or overlaps. You can count unit cubes to find the volume of a solid figure. For example, the rectangular prism above contains 6 unit cubes, so it has a volume of 6 cubic units.

Example 2

What is the volume of the rectangular prism below?

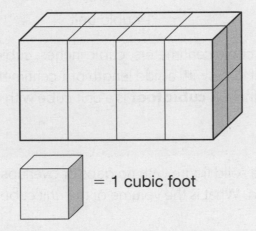

= 1 cubic foot

| **Strategy** | **Count the number of unit cubes in each layer of the prism.** |

Step 1   Count the number of unit cubes in the bottom layer.

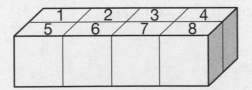

There are 8 unit cubes in the bottom layer.

Step 2   Count the number of unit cubes in the top layer of the prism.

The top layer of the prism has the same number of unit cubes as the bottom layer.

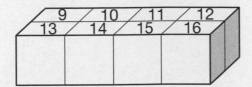

Start counting at 9 cubes.
There are 16 total unit cubes.

Step 3 Find the volume of the prism.

There are 16 unit cubes in the solid figure.

Each unit cube is 1 cubic foot.

16 unit cubes = 16 cubic feet

Solution The volume of the rectangular prism is 16 cubic feet.

Example 3

Find the volume of the solid figure. Each unit cube is 1 cubic centimeter.

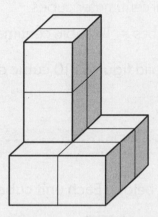

Strategy Separate the solid figure into two rectangular prisms, and count the number of unit cubes.

Step 1 Separate the solid into two rectangular prisms.

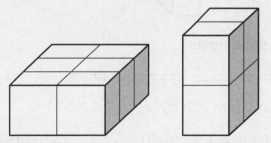

Step 2 Count the number of centimeter cubes in one prism.

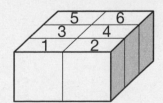

There are 6 centimeter cubes in the prism.

Step 3   Count the number of centimeter cubes in the other prism.

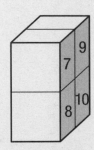

Start counting at 7 cubes.
There are 10 total centimeter cubes.

Step 4   Find the volume of the solid.

There are 10 total centimeter cubes.

10 centimeter cubes = 10 cubic centimeters

Solution   The volume of the solid figure is 10 cubic centimeters.

2 COACHED EXAMPLE

Keiko built the solid figure shown below. Each unit cube is 1 cubic inch.

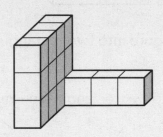

What is the volume of the solid figure?

First, separate the figure into _____ rectangular prisms.

Next, _____ the number of inch cubes.

For the rectangular prism on the left, there are _____ inch cubes.

For the rectangular prism on the right, start counting at _____,

and count _____ inch cubes in all.

There are _____ inch cubes in the solid figure.

_____ inch cubes = _____ cubic inches

The volume of the solid figure is _____.

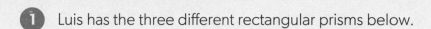
1 Luis has the three different rectangular prisms below.

Prism A   Prism B   Prism C

Which statement is correct? Circle all that apply.

A. Prism B has a greater volume than Prism C.

B. The volume of Prism C is less than the volume of Prism A.

C. The volume of Prism A is 9 cubic units.

D. Prism B has the greatest volume.

E. Prism A has the least volume.

F. Prism A and Prism C have the same volume.

2 Seth used 1-inch cubes to build the solid figure on the right. Find the volume of the solid figure.

_____ cubic inches

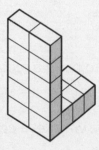

3 Jade started packing the box shown below with 1-centimeter cubes.

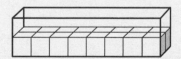

Select Yes or No for each statement.

A. Jade packed 16 cubes in the bottom of the box. ○ Yes ○ No

B. Jade needs to add 2 more layers to fill the box. ○ Yes ○ No

C. The volume of the box is 24 cubic centimeters. ○ Yes ○ No

D. The volume of the box is 32 cubic centimeters. ○ Yes ○ No

4 Zeke made the solid figure below out of inch cubes.

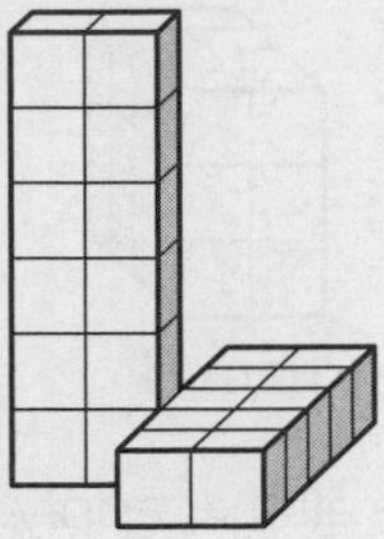

Find the volume of Zeke's solid figure. Use the numbers from the box to make the statements true.

The left rectangular prism has _____ cubes.

The right rectangular prism has _____ cubes.

The volume of the figure is _____ cubic inches.

10
12
20
22
24

5 Reva needs to build a rectangular prism with a volume of 20 cubic centimeters.

Part A

Describe one way Reva could have made the rectangular prism. Use words, numbers, or a drawing.

Part B

Describe another way Reva could have made the rectangular prism. Use words, numbers, or a drawing.

6 Use the measurements from the box to write the volume of each rectangular prism.

6 cubic inches	6 cubic centimeters	8 cubic centimeters

8 cubic feet	9 cubic inches	9 cubic feet

Rectangular Prism	Number of Unit Cubes in One Layer	Number of Layers	Unit Cube	Volume
A	4	2	centimeter	
B	3	3	inch	
C	2	4	foot	

7 Find the volume of each figure. Write the letter of the figure in the correct box. Each cube in the figures is 1 cubic foot.

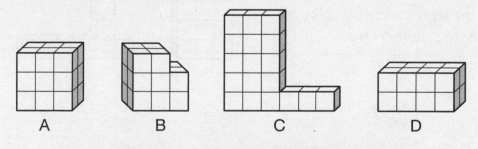

A   B   C   D

16 Cubic Feet	18 Cubic Feet

8 Ethan drew the bottom layer of a rectangular prism.

Select True or False for each statement.

A. The volume is at least 14 cubic units.　　○ True　○ False

B. Each unit cube is 3 cubic units.　　　　○ True　○ False

C. The volume of 2 layers is 28 cubic units.　○ True　○ False

D. The volume of 3 layers is 31 cubic units.　○ True　○ False

9 Olivia made a list of clues that can be used to find the volume of a rectangular prism. The clues she wrote are shown below.

- side length of each cube: 1 inch
- width of each layer: 5 unit cubes
- length of each layer: 6 unit cubes
- number of layers: 3

The volume of the rectangular prism is _____.

10 Aida built the three solid figures using inch cubes.

Circle the letters and numbers that make each statement true.

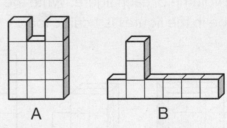
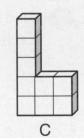

A　　　　　　B　　　　　　C

	A		5	
Figure	B	has a volume of	7	cubic inches.
	C		9	

	A			9	
Figure	B	has the	greatest / least	10	cubic inches.
	C		volume at	11	

5.MD.5.a, 5.MD.5.b

Volume of Rectangular Prisms

You know you can find the **volume** of a **rectangular prism** by counting the number of unit cubes packed in the prism. Another way is to multiply the **edge lengths**. The edge lengths are the length, width, and height of the rectangular prism.

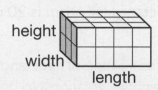

Example 1

Find the volume of the rectangular prism.

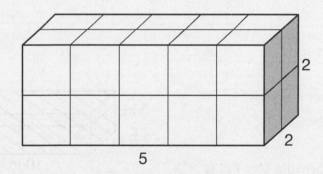

Strategy   Multiply the edge lengths of the prism.

Step 1   Determine the length, width, and height of the prism.

length = 5 unit cubes

width = 2 unit cubes

height = 2 unit cubes

Step 2   Multiply length × width × height to find the volume.

Volume = 5 × 2 × 2

= 10 × 2

= 20

Volume = 20 cubic units

Step 3   Count unit cubes to check your answer.

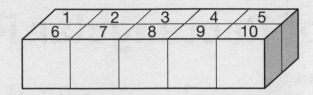

Each layer has 10 unit cubes and there are 2 layers.

10 + 10 = 20 unit cubes

The volume is 20 cubic units.

Solution   The volume of the rectangular prism is 20 cubic units.

You can also use a **formula** to find the volume of a rectangular prism. A formula is a special type of equation that shows a mathematical relationship between **variables**. In the volume formula below, l represents the length, w represents the width, and h represents the height of a rectangular prism.

Volume = length $\times$ width $\times$ height

$V = l \times w \times h$

Example 2

Layla bought a box for her markers.
Find the volume of the box.

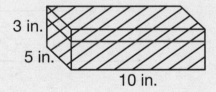

3 in.
5 in.
10 in.

Strategy   Use the formula $V = l \times w \times h$.

Step 1   Identify the variables in the formula, and replace them with the edge lengths from the box.

$$V = l \times w \times h \left\}\begin{array}{l} V = \text{volume} \\ l = \text{length} \\ w = \text{width} \\ h = \text{height} \end{array}\right.$$

Use the labels on the box. The length is 10 inches, the width is 5 inches, and the height is 3 inches.

$V = l \times w \times h$

$V = 10 \times 5 \times 3$

| Step 2 | Multiply to solve. |

$$V = 10 \times 5 \times 3$$
$$= 50 \times 3$$
$$= 150$$

Solution **The volume of the box is 150 cubic inches.**

There is another formula you can use to find the volume of a rectangular prism. In the volume formula below, B represents the **area** of the **base** of the prism, and h represents its height. The base of a rectangular prism is one of its faces. The area of the base is length $\times$ width.

Volume = Base area $\times$ height

$$V = B \times h$$

Example 3

Victor filled a flower pot to the top with soil. How many cubic centimeters of soil did Victor use to fill the pot?

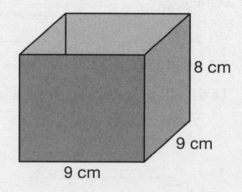

8 cm

9 cm

9 cm

Strategy **Use the formula $V = B \times h$.**

| Step 1 | Identify the variables in the formula, and replace them with the edge lengths from the pot. |

$$V = B \times h \left\{ \begin{array}{l} V = \text{volume} \\ B = \text{area of base} \\ h = \text{height} \end{array} \right.$$

Use the labels on the pot. The length is 9 cm, the width is 9 cm, and the height is 8 cm.

$$V = B \times h \qquad \text{The area of the base is length} \times \text{width.}$$
$$V = (9 \times 9) \times 8$$

| Step 2 | Multiply to solve. |

$$V = (9 \times 9) \times 8$$
$$= 81 \times 8$$
$$= 648$$

Solution **Victor used 648 cubic centimeters of soil to fill the pot.**

Ms. Lee put leftover lasagna in the container shown below.

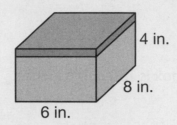

4 in.

8 in.

6 in.

What is the volume of the container?

Write a formula that can be used to find the volume of the container. _____

Identify the variables in the formula. _____

_____

What are the edge lengths of the container?

    length = _____

    width = _____

    height = _____

Use the formula to find the volume of the container. Show your work.

    $V =$ _____

      $=$ _____

      $=$ _____

      $=$ _____

The volume of the container is _____.

❶ Nadia built a rectangular prism with the same volume as the prism below.

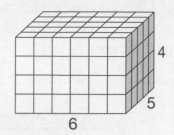

Could the measurements be the rectangular prism that Nadia built? Select Yes or No.

A. length = 8, width = 10, height = 2   ◯ Yes   ◯ No

B. length = 10, width = 4, height = 3   ◯ Yes   ◯ No

C. length = 12, width = 2, height = 10   ◯ Yes   ◯ No

D. length = 15, width = 4, height = 2   ◯ Yes   ◯ No

❷ Adam stacked some wooden boards into piles. Each board has the same dimensions.

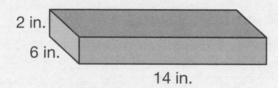

Circle the numbers that make the statement true.

	4			2	
A pile of	5	boards is		3	times the volume of a pile of 3 boards.
	6			4	

❸ Lily hid a house key in the metal box below.

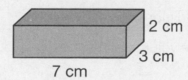

The volume of the key box is _____ cubic centimeters.

4 Diego has 60 one-inch cubes of cheese. Diego needs to place all of the cubes of cheese into a container so that it is completely filled, with no gaps. Determine if each container is too small, the exact size, or too large to fit the cubes of cheese. Write the letter of the container in the correct box.

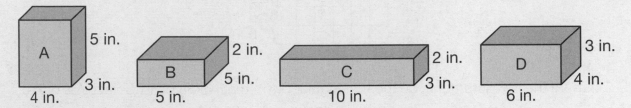

Too Small	Exact Size	Too Large

5 Hunter and Alexa used two different formulas to find the volume of the rectangular prism shown. Hunter says the volume is 25 cubic meters. Alexa says the volume is 30 cubic meters. Which student made an error in calculating the volume? _____

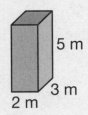

What is the possible error? Use formulas and words to explain your reasoning.

6 The locker in a gym has the dimensions shown.

Write an equation to find the volume of the locker.

$V = $ _____

The volume of the locker is _____.

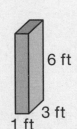

7 A company shipped crates of puzzle boxes to different stores. The puzzle box is shown.

Use the numbers from the box to write the volume of each crate. Each crate is full, with no empty spaces.

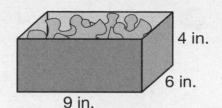

4 in.

6 in.

9 in.

824

864

1,266

1,296

1,728

Crate	Number of Puzzle Boxes	Volume of Crate (cubic in.)
A	4	
B	6	
C	8	

8 Beth packed cartons of chicken broth into different-sized packs and crates. Each carton of broth is the same size. Select True or False for each statement.

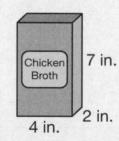

Chicken Broth

7 in.

2 in.

4 in.

A. A carton of chicken broth has a volume of 56 cubic inches.   ○ True ○ False

B. A 4-carton pack of broth has a volume of 224 cubic inches.   ○ True ○ False

C. A 6-carton pack of broth has a volume of 326 cubic inches.   ○ True ○ False

D. A crate filled with two 8-carton packs of broth has a volume of 896 cubic inches.   ○ True ○ False

9 Devin made the sand candle shown.

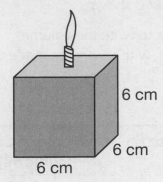

6 cm

6 cm

6 cm

Devin made another sand candle with edge lengths of 12 centimeters each. He said the side lengths of the second candle are twice the edge lengths of the first candle, so the volume of the second candle is twice the volume of the first candle. Do you agree with Devin? Explain your reasoning using words and numbers.

10 Maria used glass blocks in a craft project. The volume of each glass block is 968 cubic centimeters.

What is the height of the glass block?

_____ centimeters

Explain how you found the height. Justify your answer.

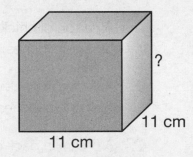

?

11 cm

11 cm

Adding Volumes of Rectangular Prisms

5.MD.5.c

1 GETTING THE IDEA

Solid figures can be made by stacking or connecting **rectangular prisms**.

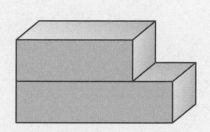

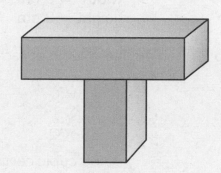

To find the volume of these solid figures:

- First, look for rectangular prisms. Remember, a rectangular prism is a solid figure with faces that are rectangles.

- Next, use a formula to find the volume of each prism.

- Last, add the volumes. The sum is the volume of the solid figure.

Example 1

Find the volume of the solid figure shown below.

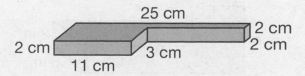

25 cm
2 cm
2 cm
2 cm
3 cm
11 cm

Strategy   Use a formula and addition to find the volume.

Step 1   Look for two rectangular prisms.

Separate the solid figure into two rectangular prisms.

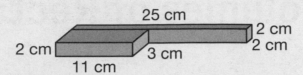

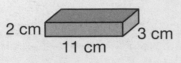

length = 11 cm
width = 3 cm
height = 2 cm

length = 25 cm
width = 2 cm
height = 2 cm

Step 2   Find the volume of each prism.

$V = l \times w \times h$

$= 11 \times 3 \times 2$

$= 33 \times 2$

$= 66$ cubic centimeters

$V = l \times w \times h$

$= 25 \times 2 \times 2$

$= 50 \times 2$

$= 100$ cubic centimeters

Step 3   Add the volumes.

Total volume = 66 + 100

= 166 cubic centimeters

Solution   The volume of the solid figure is 166 cubic centimeters.

Example 2

Kristin stacked two gifts.

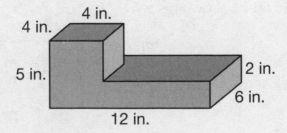

Find the total volume of the two gifts.

Strategy   Use a formula and addition to find the volume.

Step 1   Look for two rectangular prisms.

Separate the solid figure into two rectangular prisms.

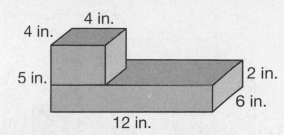

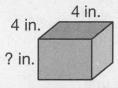

length = 4 in.   length = 12 in.
width = 4 in.   width = 6 in.
height = ? in.   height = 2 in.

Step 2   Find any unknown side lengths.

The height of the top prism is unknown.

The height of the solid figure is 5 inches, and the height of the bottom prism is 2 inches.

So, subtract to find the height.

5 inches − 2 inches = 3 inches

length = 4 inches

width = 4 inches

height = 3 inches

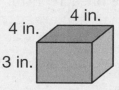

Step 3   Find the volume of each prism.

$V = l \times w \times h$ $V = l \times w \times h$

    $= 4 \times 4 \times 3$ $= 12 \times 6 \times 2$

    $= 16 \times 3$ $= 72 \times 2$

    $= 48$ cubic inches $= 144$ cubic inches

Step 4   Add the volumes.

Total volume = 48 + 144

              = 192 cubic inches

Solution   **The total volume of the two gifts is 192 cubic inches.**

Mr. Curtis has a workshop. He has a storage unit attached to the workshop, shown below.

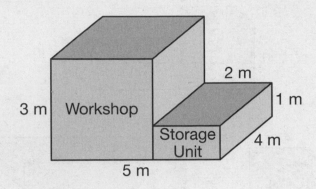

What is the total volume of the workshop and the storage unit?

First, separate the solid figure into two _____.

Determine the side lengths of each prism.

Workshop

length = _____ m

width = _____ m

height = _____ m

Storage Unit

length = _____ m

width = _____ m

height = _____ m

Find the volume of each prism.

Workshop

$V =$ _____ × _____ × _____

    = _____ × _____

    = _____ cubic meters

Storage Unit

$V =$ _____ × _____ × _____

    = _____ × _____

    = _____ cubic meters

Add to find the total volume.

_____ + _____ = _____ cubic meters

The total volume of the workshop and the storage unit is _____ cubic meters.

1   Ms. James made a metal sculpture.

Select True or False for each statement.

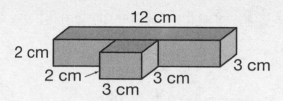

12 cm

2 cm   3 cm

2 cm   3 cm

3 cm

A.   The volume of the larger part is 72 cubic centimeters.   ○ True   ○ False

B.   The volume of the smaller part is 27 cubic centimeters.   ○ True   ○ False

C.   The total volume of the sculpture is 83 cubic centimeters.   ○ True   ○ False

D.   The larger part is 4 times the volume of the smaller part.   ○ True   ○ False

2   Adam stacked two boards. Each board has the same height and width, but different lengths. What is the total volume of the two boards? Justify your answer.

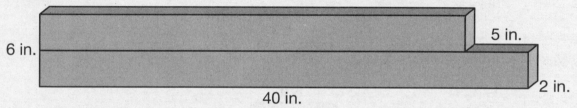

6 in.

5 in.

2 in.

40 in.

3   Elise made the wooden stamp shown below.

The volume of the stamp is _____ cubic centimeters.

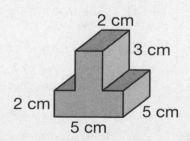

2 cm

3 cm

2 cm

5 cm

5 cm

4 Find the volume of each figure.

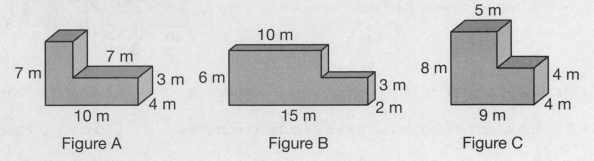

Figure A   Figure B   Figure C

Circle the letters of the figures and number that make the statement true.

A	34	
B	56	
C	150	

The volume of Figure [A B C] is [34 56 150] cubic meters greater than Figure [A B C].

5 Martin is putting the boxes shown below in a truck.

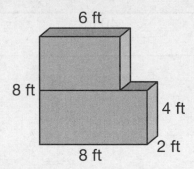

Select Yes or No for each statement.

A. The side lengths of the top box are 6 feet, 2 feet, and 4 feet. ○ Yes ○ No

B. The volume of the bottom box is 128 cubic feet. ○ Yes ○ No

C. The volume of the top box is 16 cubic feet. ○ Yes ○ No

D. The total volume of the boxes is 112 cubic feet. ○ Yes ○ No

6 Ms. Gomez bought a container to plant flowers.

She can buy potting soil in bags that are two sizes.

Find the least number of bags Ms. Gomez could buy to fill her planter. She wants to have the least amount of soil left over. Use numbers and words to explain your reasoning.

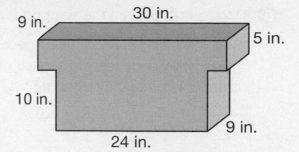

Potting Soil

Small bag = 864 cubic inches

Large bag = 1,728 cubic inches

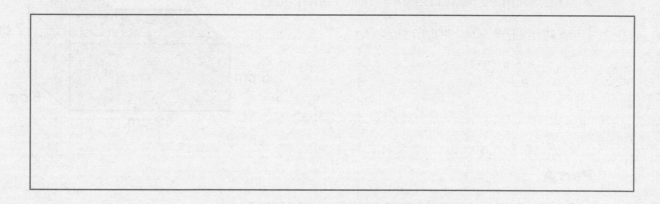

7 Use the symbols from the box to compare the volumes of the solid figures shown.

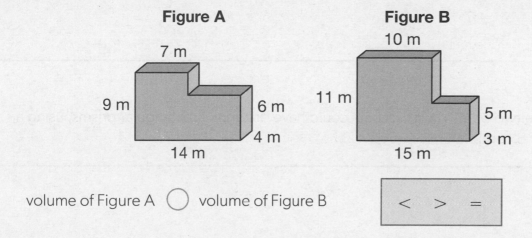

Figure A

7 m
9 m
6 m
4 m
14 m

Figure B

10 m
11 m
5 m
3 m
15 m

volume of Figure A ◯ volume of Figure B

< > =

8 Mrs. Singh bought the signpost for her yard.

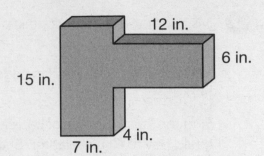

She had a carpenter increase the height of the post by 6 inches. How much greater is the volume of the new signpost?

_____ cubic inches greater

9 Mr. Parker asked his students to draw and label a solid figure. He gave these directions:

- Use two rectangular prisms.

- The volume should be 544 cubic centimeters.

Lana drew the solid figure below.

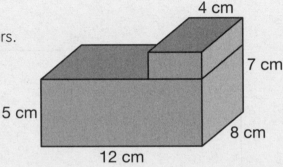

Part A

Did Lana draw a correct figure? Explain your reasoning.

Part B

Describe two other ways that Lana could have drawn the rectangular prisms, using a width of 8 centimeters.

Lola packed a box with centimeter cubes. Use the drawing for problems 1–3.

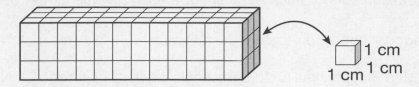

1 What did Lola measure when she packed the box with centimeter cubes? How can Lola be sure that her measurement is correct? Explain.

2 Select True or False for each statement about the cubes Lola used to pack the box.

   A. Each cube is 1 cubic centimeter.   ○ True   ○ False

   B. Each cube is 3 cubic centimeters.   ○ True   ○ False

   C. Unit cubes are always the same size.   ○ True   ○ False

   D. The total number of cubes is the volume of the box.   ○ True   ○ False

3 Find the volume of the box.

Each layer is _____ cubes long.

Each layer is _____ cubes wide.

There are _____ cubes in each layer.

There are _____ layers.

There are a total of _____ centimeter cubes.

The volume of the box is _____ cubic centimeters.

4 Mr. Yates took 3 gallons of fruit punch and 7 quarts of apple cider to a school party. He stored the refreshments in 3-quart containers. Is each statement true? Select Yes or No.

A. He needed 4 containers to store the fruit punch. ○ Yes ○ No

B. He needed 3 containers to store the apple cider. ○ Yes ○ No

C. He took 224 fluid ounces of apple cider. ○ Yes ○ No

D. He took 160 more fluid ounces of fruit punch than of apple cider. ○ Yes ○ No

5 A company makes and ships stackable crates. Each crate is in the shape of a cube. Each side length of a crate is 1 foot. The crates are packed in boxes as shown below.

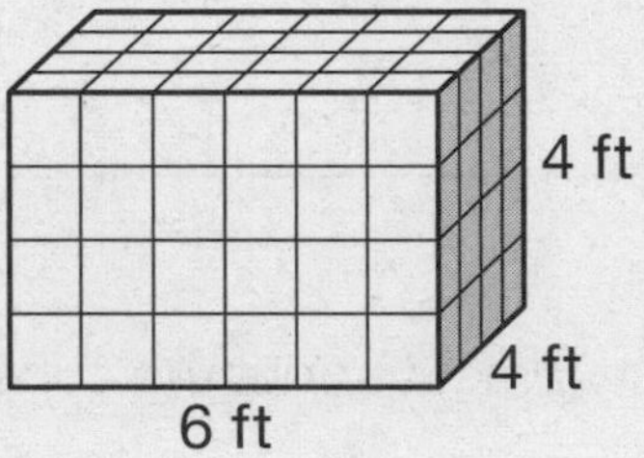

4 ft

4 ft

6 ft

Part A

Find the volume of the box. Describe the method you used to find its volume.

Part B

Describe a different method to find the volume of the box.

6 Madison measured the length of some pieces of chalk to the nearest $\frac{1}{8}$ inch. The chart shows the lengths in inches.

$2\frac{1}{2}$	3	$2\frac{5}{8}$	$2\frac{3}{4}$	$2\frac{3}{4}$	$3\frac{1}{8}$	$2\frac{3}{4}$	3
$3\frac{1}{8}$	$2\frac{3}{4}$	$3\frac{1}{4}$	$3\frac{1}{8}$	$2\frac{3}{8}$	$3\frac{1}{4}$	$2\frac{3}{4}$	$2\frac{5}{8}$
$2\frac{3}{4}$	$3\frac{1}{8}$	$2\frac{3}{8}$	$2\frac{3}{4}$	$3\frac{1}{8}$	$3\frac{1}{8}$	3	$2\frac{1}{2}$

Part A

Display the data in a line plot. Remember to label the number line. Include a title.

Part B

What is the difference in length between the longest and shortest piece of chalk? Show your work.

7 Mr. Collins replaced a section of a sidewalk at the corner of his house. He needed to find the volume of concrete he would use. He calculated the volume by finding the volume of the two sections labeled A and B.

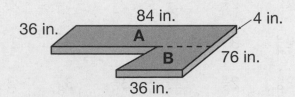

Which statement about the sidewalk is true? Circle all that apply.

A. Find $V = 84 \times 76 \times 4$ to determine the volume of one part of the sidewalk.

B. Part A is 84 inches long, 36 inches wide, and 4 inches tall.

C. The volume of one part of the sidewalk is 10,944 cubic inches.

D. The volume of Part B is 5,760 cubic inches.

E. A total of 17,856 cubic inches of concrete was needed in all.

8 Michaela sold bags of sweet potatoes at a farmer's market. She recorded the weights of the bags she sold on the line plot.

Sweet Potato Weights (in pounds)

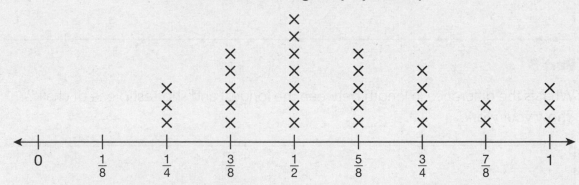

Compare the sweet potato weights. Use the symbols from the box to make each comparison true.

$$\boxed{<\quad>\quad=}$$

total weight of $\frac{5}{8}$-pound bags $\bigcirc$ total weight of $\frac{1}{2}$-pound bags

total weight of $\frac{3}{8}$-pound bags $\bigcirc$ total weight of $\frac{7}{8}$-pound bags

total weight of $\frac{3}{4}$-pound bags $\bigcirc$ total weight of 1-pound bags

total weight of $\frac{1}{4}$-pound bags $\bigcirc$ total weight of $\frac{7}{8}$-pound bags

9 Cody made two figures out of one block of clay. He used the whole block. The volume of the two figures is 360 cubic centimeters. What could be the length, width, and height of the block of clay?

Length: _____ centimeters

Width: _____ centimeters

Height: _____ centimeters

Justify that the volume of the block of clay equals the volume of the 2 figures. Write and solve a volume formula for the block of clay.

Volume of the block of clay:

$V =$ _____ = _____ = _____

The block of clay has a volume of _____ cubic centimeters.

10 Mr. Wu wants to put strings of lights on his patio. He needs 12 meters of lights in all. He can buy strings of lights in these packages:

- 225-centimeter string
- 275-centimeter string

Mr. Wu wants to get as close to 12 meters as he can without going over. How many packages should he buy of each type?

Packages of 225-centimeter strings: _____

Packages of 275-centimeter strings: _____

Use numbers and words to explain your reasoning.

Toy Robots

You make toy robots and sell them online. The robots you make vary in weight. The line plot shows the weights of the robots that have been purchased. Now, they just need to be shipped.

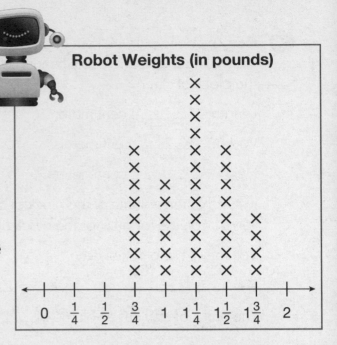

Robot Weights (in pounds)

Part A No matter how much they weigh, each robot is placed in a rectangular package that measures 1 foot on each side. What is the volume of the package? Describe the shape of the package and explain how you determined the volume.

Part B The table shows the dimensions of boxes that you use for shipping the packages of robots.

Shipping Box	Length (in inches)	Width (in inches)	Height (in inches)
A	12	12	36
B	12	24	36
C	24	24	24
D	24	24	36

Rewrite the table to show the length, width, and height of each shipping box in feet. Then find the volume of each box.

Shipping Box	Length (in feet)	Width (in feet)	Height (in feet)	Volume (in cubic feet)
A				
B				
C				
D				

Part C A toy store purchased all of your $1\frac{1}{4}$-pound robots and $1\frac{1}{2}$-pound robots. Describe how you could ship the packages using the least number of shipping boxes. Provide the weights of the robots that will be placed in each shipping box.

Part D Each shipping box can only hold 10 pounds or less. Explain why your plan from Part C no longer works. Then describe a new plan for shipping the packages. Verify that your new plan will work. Empty space in a box is allowed, but should be avoided as much as possible.

DOMAIN 5

Geometry

5.G.1

Graphing on Coordinate Planes

- -

A **coordinate plane** is a grid formed by a horizontal number line called the **x-axis** and a vertical number line called the **y-axis**. The **origin** is the point (0, 0) where the x-axis and y-axis intersect.

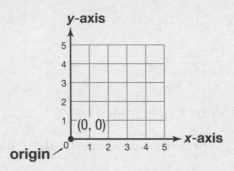

An **ordered pair** is a pair of numbers describing the location of a point on the coordinate plane. An example of an ordered pair is (2, 5).

The **x-coordinate** is the first number in an ordered pair, and it tells how many units to move along the x-axis.

The **y-coordinate** is the second number in an ordered pair, and it tells how many units to move along the y-axis.

Example 1

Write the ordered pair for point P.

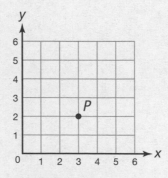

Strategy   Find the coordinates of the ordered pair.

Step 1   Find the *x*-coordinate.

Start at the origin.

Move right along the *x*-axis from the origin until you are under point *P*.

Count the number of units you moved. The *x*-coordinate is 3.

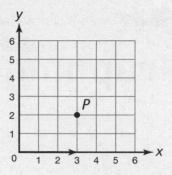

Step 2   Find the *y*-coordinate.

Move up until you reach point *P*.

Count the units you moved up on the *y*-axis. The *y*-coordinate is 2.

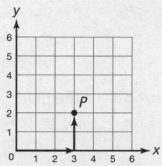

Step 3   Write the ordered pair.

(3, 2)

The *x*-coordinate corresponds to the number on the *x*-axis.   The *y*-coordinate corresponds to the number on the *y*-axis.

Solution   The ordered pair for point *P* is (3, 2).

Example 2

Plot the point (4, 5) on a coordinate plane.

Strategy   **Use the coordinates to locate the point.**

Step 1   Find how many units to move from the origin along the *x*-axis.

The *x*-coordinate is 4.

Start at the origin. Move 4 units to the right along the *x*-axis.

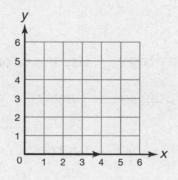

Step 2   Find how many units to move up from the x-axis.

The y-coordinate is 5. Move up 5 units.

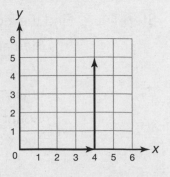

Step 3   Plot the point.

Plot a point at (4, 5). Label the point with the ordered pair.

Solution   The point (4, 5) is shown on the coordinate plane in Step 3.

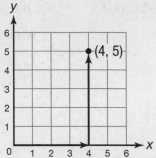

Example 3

Name the point for the ordered pair (2, 4).

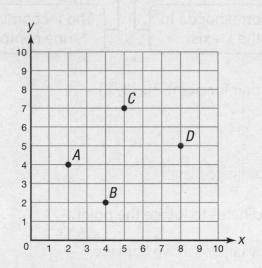

Strategy   Use the coordinates to locate the point on the coordinate plane.

Step 1   Identify the x- and y-coordinates in the ordered pair.

The x-coordinate is 2. The y-coordinate is 4.

Step 2   Find the point with the given coordinates.

Find 2 on the x-axis and 4 on the y-axis. Follow the lines that extend from each axis until they intersect. The lines intersect at point A.

Solution   Point A names the ordered pair (2, 4).

Name the point for the ordered pair (6, 2).

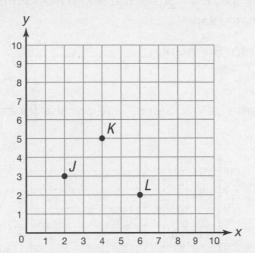

The x-coordinate is _____.

The y-coordinate is _____.

Follow the line extending from _____ on the x-axis.

Follow the line extending from _____ on the y-axis.

The lines intersect at point _____.

Point _____ names the ordered pair (6, 2).

1 A point is located 8 units to the right of the origin along the *x*-axis and 1 unit up along the *y*-axis on a coordinate plane.

Write the ordered pair for the point. (_____ , _____)

2 Use the coordinate plane below. Select True or False for each statement.

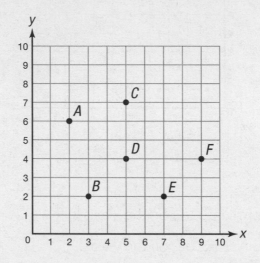

A. The *y*-coordinate for point *A* is 6. ○ True ○ False

B. Point *B* has the same *x*-coordinate as point *E*. ○ True ○ False

C. The *x*-coordinate for point *C* is 5. ○ True ○ False

D. The ordered pair for point *F* is (9, 4). ○ True ○ False

E. Point *D* names the ordered pair (4, 5). ○ True ○ False

3 Point *A* is located at (5, 8) on a coordinate plane. What is the ordered pair for a point that is 2 units below point *A*? Select one number from each column to form the ordered pair (*x*, *y*).

3	6
(5 , 8)
7	10

4 Plot the points on the coordinate plane.

J(2, 8), K(7, 4), L(3, 5), M(5, 2)

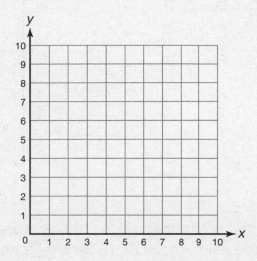

5 Use the coordinate plane below.

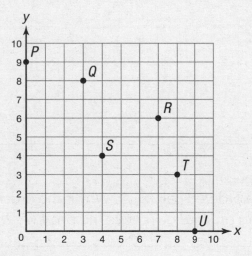

Name the point located at (8, 3). _____

What is the ordered pair for point R? (_____, _____)

Which point is on the y-axis? _____

What is the ordered pair for point U? (_____, _____)

6 Which ordered pair locates a point on the coordinate plane shown? Circle all that apply.

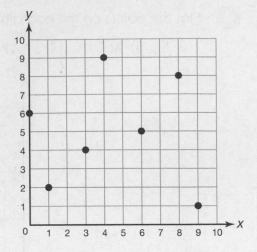

A. (6, 0)   D. (2, 1)

B. (4, 9)   E. (8, 9)

C. (3, 4)   F. (6, 5)

7 Point Z is 5 units to the right of the origin along the x-axis and 1 unit up the y-axis. Lutz says that the ordered pair for point Z is (1, 5). Is he correct? Explain.

8 Explain how to plot the ordered pair (2, 7). Why is the order of the coordinates important when plotting ordered pairs? Use the point (7, 2) in your explanation.

9 Use the descriptions to plot each point on the coordinate plane.

- Point *D* is 4 units right and 5 units up from the origin.
- Point *E* is 2 units right and 3 units down from point *D*.
- Point *F* has the same *x*-coordinate as point *E* and a *y*-coordinate of 8.
- Point *G* has the same *y*-coordinate as point *F* and an *x*-coordinate of 1.

Write the ordered pairs for the points you graphed.

point *D* (_____, _____)

point *E* (_____, _____)

point *F* (_____, _____)

point *G* (_____, _____)

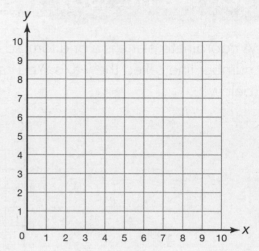

10 Select the ordered pair that makes each statement true.

(0, 1)

(1, 1)   is located on the *x*-axis.

(1, 0)

(5, 0)

(0, 5)   is located on the *y*-axis.

(5, 5)

(1, 5)

(6, 0)   is located 5 units to the right and 1 unit up from

(5, 1)

(0, 0)

(1, 1) .

(5, 5)

Solving Problems with Coordinate Planes

 GETTING THE IDEA

A coordinate plane is a grid formed by a horizontal number line called the *x*-axis and a vertical number line called the *y*-axis. You can use a coordinate plane as a map, like the one shown below.

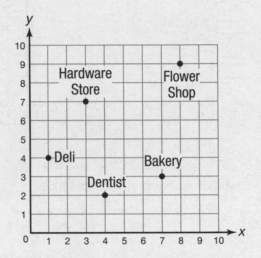

You can use directions to describe locations on the map.

- The bakery is 7 units to the right of the origin and 3 units up from the *x*-axis.

- The hardware store is 2 units to the right and 3 units up from the deli.

Coordinate planes can also be used as blueprints or for many other things that use ordered pairs.

Example 1

A map of the county fairgrounds is shown below. The entrance to the fair is located at the origin. If you begin at the entrance and walk first along the x-axis, how far will you walk to reach the games?

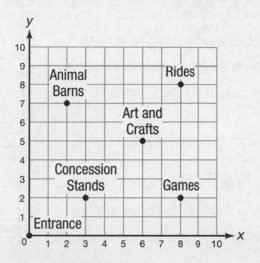

Strategy   Use coordinates to determine the distanced walked.

Step 1   Find the coordinates of the games.

The games are located at (8, 2).

Step 2   Describe the location.

Start at the origin. Since the x-coordinate is 8, walk 8 units to the right.

The y-coordinate is 2, so walk 2 units up.

Step 3   Find the distance to the games.

Add the units: 8 + 2 = 10.

Solution   You will walk 10 units to get from the entrance to the games.

Example 2

Julie is drawing a map of her town. Follow the directions to complete Julie's map.

- The school is at (4, 1).

- The bank is at (2, 3).

- The library is 4 units up from the bank.

- The post office is 6 units to the right of the library.

- The fire station is 5 units to the right and 1 unit up from the school.

Strategy   Plot points on a coordinate plane.

Step 1 Plot the locations with known coordinates.

The coordinates for the school are (4, 1).

Start at the origin. Move 4 units to the right and 1 unit up.

Plot and label a point for the school.

The coordinates for the bank are (2, 3).

Start at the origin. Move 2 units to the right and 3 units up.

Plot and label the point for the bank.

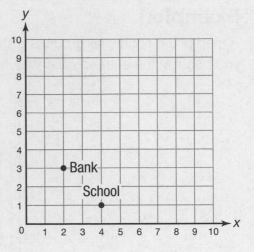

Step 2 Find the location of the library.

The library is 4 units up from the bank.

Start at the coordinates for the bank at (2, 3).

Move 4 units up.

Plot and label a point for the library at (2, 7).

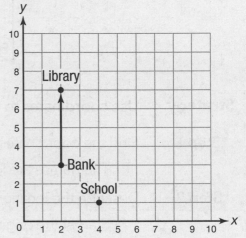

Step 3 Find the location of the post office.

The post office is 6 units to the right of the library.

Start at the coordinates for the library at (2, 7).

Move 6 units to the right.

Plot and label a point for the post office at (8, 7).

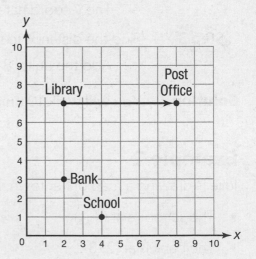

Step 4 Find the location of the fire station.

The fire station is 5 units to the right and 1 unit up from the school.

Start at the coordinates for the school at (4, 1).

Move 5 units to the right and 1 unit up.

Plot and label a point for the fire station at (9, 2).

Solution The map of Julie's town is shown in Step 4.

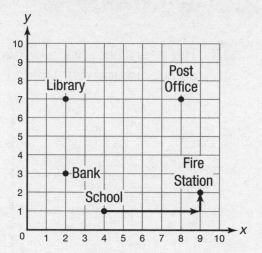

❷ COACHED EXAMPLE

Dante is drawing a map of the library shown. He has drawn the locations for the audio books section at (2, 1) and the reading area at (5, 5).

Follow the directions to complete the map. Draw and label the missing points on the map.

- The fiction section is 7 units up from the audio books section.

- The nonfiction section is 6 units to the right of the fiction section.

- The children's books section is 3 units to the right and 3 units down from the reading area.

To find the location of the fiction section, start at (_____, _____).

Move 7 units _____. Plot and label a point for the fiction section at (_____, _____).

To find the location of the nonfiction section, start at (_____, _____).

Move 6 units _____. Plot and label a point for the nonfiction section at (_____, _____).

To find the location of the children's book section, start at (_____, _____).

Move _____ units right and 3 units _____. Plot and label a point for the children's

books section at (_____, _____).

Label the points on the map above.

1 The coordinate plane below shows the location of several items found at an archaeological dig. Select True or False for each statement.

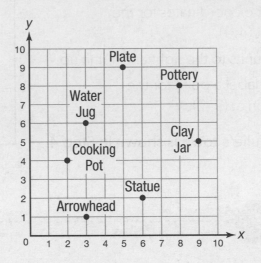

A. A statue is at (2, 6). ○ True ○ False

B. The arrowhead is 5 units down from the water jug. ○ True ○ False

C. The clay jar is 9 units from the *x*-axis. ○ True ○ False

D. A plate is at (5, 9). ○ True ○ False

E. The cooking pot and clay jar have the same *y*-coordinate. ○ True ○ False

2 Plot the points on the coordinate plane. Connect the points in the order they have been given. What letter is formed?

(2, 2), (2, 5), (2, 8), (7, 2), (7, 5), (7, 8)

Letter: _____

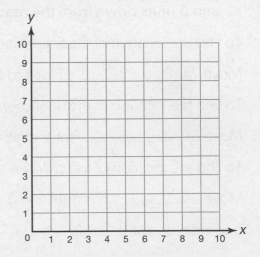

3 Miguel's school is located at (4, 2) on a map. After school, Miguel walked 2 blocks north (up) and 3 blocks to the east (right), to reach the bookstore. What is the ordered pair that names the location of the bookstore?

Select one number from each column to form the ordered pair (x, y) for the bookstore.

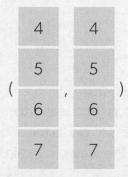

4 Olivia is using the park map shown below.

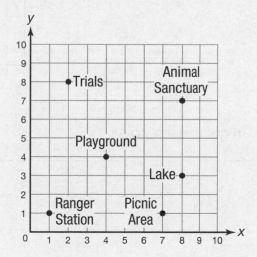

What is the ordered pair for the location of the animal sanctuary? (_____, _____)

What is located at (4, 4)? _____

How far is the picnic area from the ranger station? _____

5 Luke draws a square on a coordinate plane. One vertex is located at (1, 2), and the length of each side is 6 units. Look at each ordered pair. Can the ordered pair be one of the vertices of the square? Select Yes or No.

A. (6, 6)　　○ Yes　○ No　　　　**C.** (7, 2)　　○ Yes　○ No

B. (6, 7)　　○ Yes　○ No　　　　**D.** (7, 8)　　○ Yes　○ No

6 The coordinate plane shows a map of a playground. Sophia is at the swings. She wants to go to the sandbox. Then, she plans to go to the slide. Finally, she will meet her sister at the water fountain.

Part A

Describe how Sophia can get to each point.

Part B

How many total units will she walk? Show your work.

7 Which ordered pair locates a point on the map of the farm? Circle all that apply.

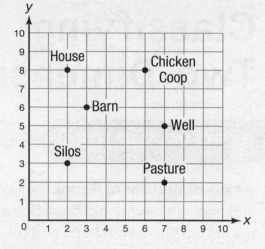

A. (2, 8)   D. (6, 8)

B. (3, 2)   E. (7, 5)

C. (3, 6)   F. (7, 8)

8 Use the descriptions to plot each point on the map of a carnival.

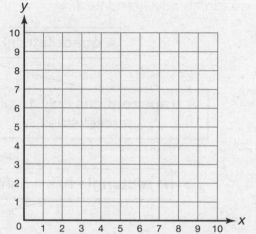

• The carousel is located at (2, 2).

• The fun house is 4 units to the right and 1 unit up from the carousel.

• The roller coaster is 2 units to the right and 2 units up from the fun house.

• The water slide is 7 units to the left and 1 unit up from the roller coaster.

• The Ferris wheel is 2 units up and 4 units to the right of the water slide.

9 Plot the points given below on the coordinate plane. Connect the points in the order they have been given. Be sure to connect point *D* back to point *A*.

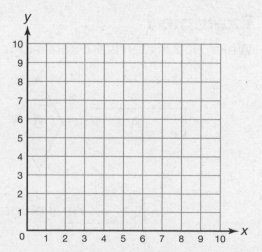

A(2, 8), *B*(8, 8), *C*(8, 5), *D*(2, 5)

What is the perimeter of the figure? _____ units

What is the area of the figure? _____ square units

5.G.3, 5.G.4

Classifying Two-Dimensional Figures

1 GETTING THE IDEA

A **two-dimensional figure** is a flat figure that can be measured in two ways, such as length and width. It has no thickness. Some two-dimensional figures are polygons. A **polygon** is a closed figure with three or more line segments as sides. This diagram shows how quadrilaterals are related.

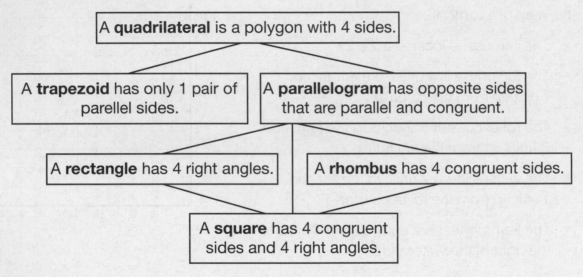

Example 1

Which quadrilaterals are parallelograms? Write the letter for each figure in the correct box.

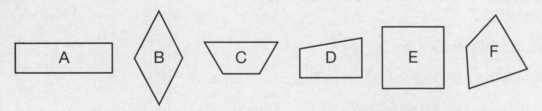

Parallelogram	Not a Parallelogram

Strategy   Use the properties of parallelograms to classify each figure.

Step 1   Eliminate figures that do **not** have parallel sides.

Parallel sides never intersect.

Figures C and D have only 1 pair of parallel sides. Figures C and D are not parallelograms. They are both trapezoids.

Figure F has no parallel sides. It is a quadrilateral that is not a parallelogram or a trapezoid.

Step 2   Check the remaining figures for parallel sides.

Figures A, B, and E all have 2 pairs of parallel sides. Figures A, B, and E are parallelograms.

Step 3   Fill in the table.

Parallelogram	Not a Parallelogram
A B E	C D F

Solution   Figures A, B, and E are parallelograms. The table is shown in Step 3.

Example 2

Which quadrilateral has 2 right angles and only 1 pair of parallel sides? Name the figure.

     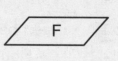

Strategy   Compare quadrilaterals with the properties listed to classify each figure.

Step 1   Look for quadrilaterals with right angles.

Figures A, B, and E have right angles. All of these figures have at least 2 right angles.

Step 2   Out of the figures with 2 or more right angles, look for figures that have only 1 pair of parallel sides.

Figures A and E have 2 pairs of parallel sides. Figure B has its vertical sides parallel, but the other 2 sides are not parallel.

Step 3   Name the figure.

Figure B has 2 right angles and only 1 pair of parallel sides.

Figure B is a trapezoid.

Solution   **Figure B is a trapezoid that has 2 right angles and 1 pair of parallel sides.**

Example 3

Where would you place each figure in the diagram?

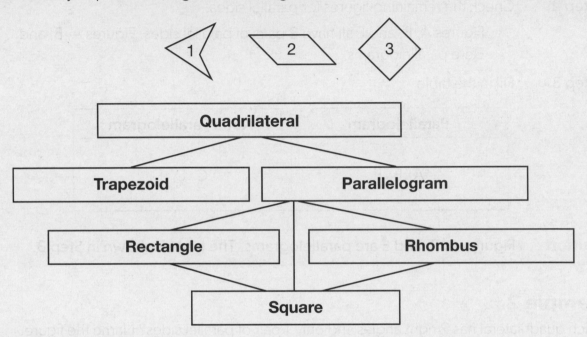

Strategy   Use the properties of quadrilaterals to classify each figure.

Step 1   Describe the properties of each figure.

Figure 1 has 4 sides. It has no right angles and no parallel sides.

Figure 2 has 4 sides with opposite sides parallel and congruent. It cannot be a square or rhombus because its sides are not equal and it has no right angles.

Figure 3 has 4 congruent sides and 4 right angles.

Step 2   Determine where to place each figure in the diagram.

Figure 1 is a quadrilateral with no special characteristics.

Figure 2 is a parallelogram since it has no right angles.

Figure 3 is a square because it has 4 congruent sides and 4 right angles.

Solution   **Figure 1 is a quadrilateral. Figure 2 is a parallelogram. Figure 3 is a square.**

Example 4

Use the figures in Example 3. Give all possible names for each figure.

Strategy   Compare the properties of each figure for each category of quadrilaterals.

Step 1   What properties does Figure 1 have?

Figure 1 is a quadrilateral with no parallel sides. It may have 2 congruent sides, but they are not opposite sides.

Step 2   What properties does Figure 2 have?

Figure 2 is a parallelogram because it has parallel sides that are also congruent. It has 4 sides, so it is also a quadrilateral.

Step 3   What properties does Figure 3 have?

Figure 3 is a square because it has parallel sides that are congruent and 4 right angles.

It is also a parallelogram because it has parallel sides that are congruent.

It is also a rectangle because it is a parallelogram and it has 4 right angles.

It is also a rhombus because it is a parallelogram with 4 congruent sides.

And it is also a quadrilateral because it has 4 sides.

Solution   The names for each figure are shown in each step.

② COACHED EXAMPLE

Classify the figure below in as many ways as you can.

The figure has _____ sides. So, it is a _____.

It has _____ pair(s) of congruent sides and 2 pairs of _____ sides.

So, it is a _____.

It also has 4 _____ angles. That makes the figure a _____.

The figure can be classified as _____.

3 LESSON PRACTICE

1 Which word can be used to describe the figure? Circle all that apply.

A. polygon   **D.** quadrilateral

B. rhombus   **E.** trapezoid

C. parallelogram   **F.** square

2 Use the words from the box to describe the difference between a square and a rhombus.

A rhombus and a square are both _____s.

A _____ is a rhombus, but a _____ is not a square.

> square
>
> parallelogram
>
> rectangle
>
> rhombus

3 Circle the word that makes the statement true.

The figure that is a quadrilateral but **not** a parallelogram is a _____ .

> square
>
> rectangle
>
> trapezoid
>
> rhombus

4 A figure with 4 congruent sides and no right angles is a _____ . Draw the figure.

5 Select True or False for each statement about quadrilaterals.

    A. All quadrilaterals have 4 sides.   ○ True   ○ False

    B. All quadrilaterals have right angles.   ○ True   ○ False

    C. The sides of a square are congruent.   ○ True   ○ False

    D. A trapezoid is also a rectangle.   ○ True   ○ False

    E. A rhombus is also a rectangle.   ○ True   ○ False

6 Lincoln has a plot of land that is a 30-meter by 20-meter rectangle. He divides the plot into two parts by drawing a line from the middle of the longer side to one of the opposite corners. Name the shape of the larger section of land. Draw a picture, and explain your reasoning.

7 Look at the figures.

Select Yes or No for each statement about the figures.

    A. Figure V and Figure R are trapezoids.   ○ Yes   ○ No

    B. Figure W is not a parallelogram.   ○ Yes   ○ No

    C. Figure S and Figure T are rectangles.   ○ Yes   ○ No

    D. All of the figures are quadrilaterals.   ○ Yes   ○ No

    E. None of the figures is a rhombus.   ○ Yes   ○ No

8 Draw two different quadrilaterals that are **not** parallelograms. Describe the figures.

9 Zelda needs help with classifying figures. Use words, numbers, or drawings to explain your answers for each question.

Part A

Zelda says that a parallelogram and a trapezoid are the same. What is her error?

Part B

Zelda wants to know how she can tell the difference between a parallelogram and a rhombus. What would you tell her?

10 Think about the properties of each figure. Write the name of each figure in the correct box.

| square | trapezoid | parallelogram |

| rectangle | rhombus |

At Least 1 Pair of Parallel Sides	At Least 1 Right Angle

11 The table shows how some quadrilaterals are related. Write each word in the correct section of the table

| square | rectangle | rhombus |

4 congruent sides	4 right angles	4 congruent sides and 4 right angles

1 Select True or False for each statement about the coordinate plane below.

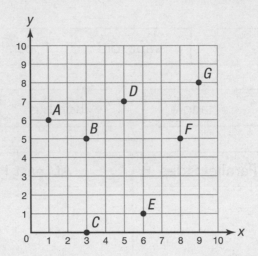

A. Point *B* has the same *x*-coordinate as point *F*.   ○ True   ○ False

B. The *x*-coordinate for point *C* is 0.   ○ True   ○ False

C. The ordered pair for point *D* is (5, 7).   ○ True   ○ False

D. Point *G* is 9 units from the *y*-axis.   ○ True   ○ False

E. Point *A* names the ordered pair (6, 1).   ○ True   ○ False

2 Think about the properties of each figure. Write the name of each figure in the correct box.

trapezoid	parallelogram	rhombus

rectangle	square

At Least 2 Congruent Sides	At Least 1 Pair of Parallel Sides

3 The locations of several animals at the zoo are shown on the map.

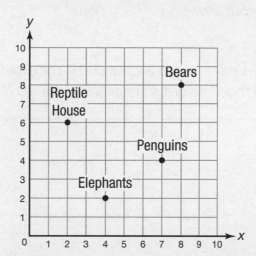

Draw a line from each animal to the description of its location.

A. Reptiles •

B. Elephants •

C. Bears •

D. Penguins •

• (4, 2)

• closest to *y*-axis

• 5 units right and 2 units down from the Reptile House

• 8 units from *x*-axis

4 On a coordinate plane, two vertices of a square are located at (3, 2) and (8, 7). Name the ordered pairs of the other two vertices of the square.

(_____ , _____)   (_____ , _____)

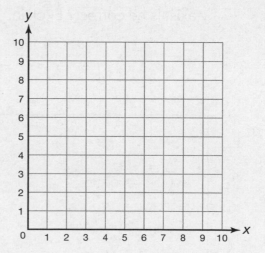

5 Dom is classifying quadrilaterals for a homework assignment. Use words, numbers, or drawings to explain your answers for each part.

Part A

Dom says that all squares have 4 right angles and 4 congruent sides. A rhombus has 4 congruent sides, so a rhombus is a square. Is she correct?

Part B

Dom drew a figure with 4 sides. It has two pairs of parallel and congruent sides. List all of the figures she could have drawn.

6 Brian says the ordered pair for point T is (4, 3), so it is 4 units from the x-axis and 3 units from the y-axis. Is he correct? Explain.

7 Use the descriptions to plot each point on the coordinate plane.

- Point *J* is 3 units right and 6 units up from the origin.
- Point *K* is 6 units right and 2 units down from point *J*.
- Point *L* has the same *x*-coordinate as point *J* and a *y*-coordinate of 2.
- Point *M* has the same *y*-coordinate as point *L* and an *x*-coordinate of 7.

Write the ordered pairs for the points you graphed.

Point *J* (_____ , _____)

Point *K* (_____ , _____)

Point *L* (_____ , _____)

Point *M* (_____ , _____)

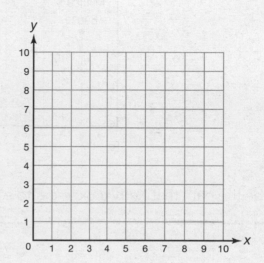

8 Select Yes or No for each statement about the figures below.

A. Figure C is a square.   ○ Yes ○ No

B. Figure B is a trapezoid.   ○ Yes ○ No

C. Figure A and Figure C are parallelograms.   ○ Yes ○ No

D. Figure D and Figure E are trapezoids.   ○ Yes ○ No

E. Figure F is a rhombus and a square.   ○ Yes ○ No

9 After school, Kerry rides her bike to the library. She checks out a book and then rides her bike to Monica's house. The girls do some homework and then decide to walk to the park.

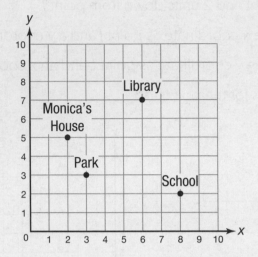

Part A

Describe the path that Kerry took to get to each location.

Part B

How many units did Kerry ride her bike? Explain how you found the answer.

Plan the Fair!

You have been asked to plan the layout of the County Fair. Use Math Tool: Plan the Fair!

• Use a coordinate grid to draw where each activity will be located.
• Each activity at the fair will have its own space.
• None of the activity spaces can overlap.

Part A The space for each activity is a quadrilateral and should be located inside the Fairground. Use the guidelines below to draw the borders of the Fairground and each activity space. Label each quadrilateral with the name of the activity.

Fairground The four vertices of the Fairground are at (0, 0), (10, 0), (10, 7), and (0, 7).

Petting Zoo Draw vertices at (4, 3), (7, 0), and (9, 0). Find the fourth vertex to make the activity space a parallelogram.

Rides This activity space should be a rectangle that covers 8 square units. One side of the activity space touches the space for Games.
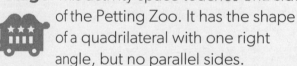

Entrance The Entrance starts at the origin. One of its vertices is at (4, 4). This activity space has the shape of a parallelogram.

Stage This activity space touches one side of the Petting Zoo. It has the shape of a quadrilateral with one right angle, but no parallel sides.

Games This activity space is a square no greater than 2 units wide. Draw one vertex of the square at (4, 4).

Prizes This activity space has the shape of a trapezoid. One of its sides touches a side of the Petting Zoo.

Part B Consider the quadrilateral you created for each activity space at the fair. In the table, place an "X" under each characteristic that applies to the quadrilateral for each activity space. The Fairground has been completed for you as an example. Which spaces are parallelograms? Explain how you know.

Part C How are the quadrilaterals for the spaces similar? How are they different? Explain.

Part D Look at your layout plan for the fair. What changes would you recommend to make better use of the entire Fairground? Explain your answer.

area the measurement of a surface or figure in square units (Lesson 26)

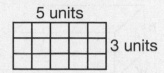

5 units

3 units

Area = 15 square units

area model a rectangular model that shows a value in square units (Lesson 12)

base (of a rectangular prism) any face of a rectangular prism (Lesson 26)

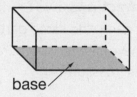

base

base (number) a number that is multiplied by itself a certain number of times (Lesson 5)

6^3

↑

base

common denominator a common multiple of two or more denominators (Lesson 14)

$\frac{1}{2}$ and $\frac{1}{4}$ have a common denominator of 4.

common multiple a multiple that two or more numbers share (Lesson 14)

multiplies of 3: 3, 6, 9, **12**, 15, . . .

multiplies of 4: 4, 8, **12**, 16, 20, . . .

multiplies of 6: 6, **12**, 18, 24, 30, . . .

3, 4, and 6 have a common multiple of 12.

convert to change a measurement given in one unit to an equivalent measurement using a larger or smaller unit (Lesson 23)

12 inches = 1 foot

1 ton = 2,000 pounds

3,000 milliliters = 3 liters

coordinate plane a grid formed by a horizontal number line called the x-axis that intersects a vertical number line called the y-axis (Lessons 3, 28)

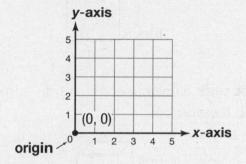

corresponding terms a pair of terms that have the same position in two sequences (Lesson 3)

cubic centimeter a unit cube with a side length of 1 centimeter (Lesson 25)

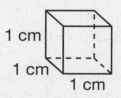

1 cm

1 cm

1 cm

cubic foot a unit cube with a side length of 1 foot (Lesson 25)

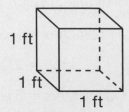

cubic inch a unit cube with a side length of 1 inch (Lesson 25)

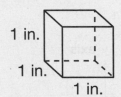

cubic unit a unit cube with a side length of 1 unit (Lesson 25)

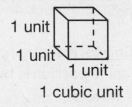

1 cubic unit

dividend the number being divided (Lessons 10, 22)

$$\frac{80}{3\overline{)240}} \leftarrow \text{dividend}$$

divisor the number by which another number is divided (Lessons 10, 21)

$$\text{divisor} \rightarrow \frac{80}{3\overline{)240}}$$

edge lengths length, width, and height of a rectangular prism (Lesson 26)

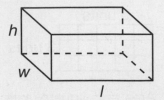

equation a number sentence that shows that the values on both sides of the equal sign are the same (Lesson 15)

$$8 \times \frac{1}{3} = \frac{8}{3}$$

equivalent fractions two or more fractions that name the same part or amount but have different numerators and denominators (Lesson 14)

$$\frac{1}{2} = \frac{2}{4} = \frac{4}{8}$$

evaluate to find the value of an expression (Lesson 2)

$$6 + 2 - 3 = 5$$

expanded form a way of writing a number as a sum of the values of its digits (Lesson 6)

308,211 in expanded form is
$300,000 + 8,000 + 200 + 10 + 2.$

exponent a number that tells how many times a given number is used as a factor (Lesson 5)

exponent

face any flat surface of a solid figure that is a polygon (Lesson 25)

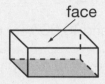

face

factor a number multiplied by another number to find a product (Lesson 9)

$$7 \times 3 = 21$$
$$\uparrow \quad \uparrow$$
$$\text{factors}$$

formula a special type of equation that shows a mathematical relationship (Lesson 26)

Volume = length $\times$ width $\times$ height

$$V = l \times w \times h$$

frequency the number of times something occurs in a data set (Lesson 24)

$$\frac{1}{8}, \frac{2}{8}, \frac{2}{8}, \frac{2}{8}, \frac{4}{8}, \frac{4}{8}, \frac{4}{8}, \frac{4}{8}, \frac{4}{8}, \frac{5}{8}, \frac{5}{8}, \frac{6}{8}, \frac{6}{8}, \frac{6}{8}, \frac{6}{8}$$

$\frac{2}{8}$ has a frequency of 3.

grouping symbols a pair of symbols used to group numbers or terms (Lesson 2)

Symbols: parentheses ( ), brackets [ ], and braces { }

$$\{4 \times [10 \div (2 + 3)] + (20 - 5) \div 3\} - 7$$

improper fraction a fraction in which the numerator is greater than or equal to the denominator (Lesson 14)

$\frac{8}{3}$ and $\frac{7}{5}$ are improper fractions.

inverse operations operations that undo each other (Lesson 21)

Multiplication and division are inverse operations.

line plot a display that uses a number line to show data; Xs are used to show frequency (Lesson 24)

mixed number a number that has a whole-number part and a fraction part (Lesson 14)

$3\frac{1}{4}$ and $6\frac{5}{9}$ are mixed numbers.

numerical expression an expression that combines numbers and at least one operation (addition, subtraction, multiplication, or division) (Lesson 1)

$$3 + 5$$

order of operations an agreed-on set of rules that indicates the order in which to calculate in an expression (Lesson 2)

1. Perform operations inside grouping symbols.

2. Multiply and divide from left to right.

3. Add and subtract from left to right.

$$(8 + 12) \times (6 - 3) = 20 \times 2 = 40$$

ordered pair a pair of numbers describing the location of a point on the coordinate plane (Lessons 3, 28)

$$(3, 5)$$

origin the point (0, 0) where the *x*-axis and *y*-axis of a coordinate plane intersect (Lesson 28)

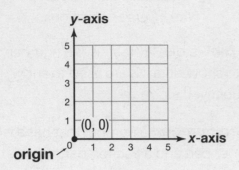

parallelogram a quadrilateral with opposite sides parallel and congruent (Lesson 30)

partial product the result of multiplying one factor by the ones, tens, hundreds, and so on of the other factor (Lesson 9)

$$\begin{array}{r} 15 \\ \times\, 13 \\ \hline 45 \\ +\, 150 \\ \hline 195 \end{array}$$ ← partial products

polygon a closed figure with three or more line segments as sides (Lesson 30)

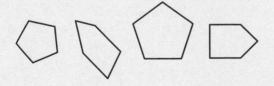

power of 10 a value represented by multiplying 10 by itself a certain number of times (Lesson 5)

100; 1,000; and 10,000 are powers of 10.

product the result of multiplying two or more numbers, or factors (Lesson 9)

$$2 \times 20 = 40$$
↑
product

quadrilateral a polygon with four sides (Lesson 30)

quotient the result when dividing a dividend by a divisor (Lessons 10, 21)

$$\begin{array}{r} 80 \\ 3\overline{)240} \end{array}$$ ← quotient

reciprocal one of two numbers whose product is 1 (Lesson 21)

$\frac{2}{3}$ and $\frac{3}{2}$ are reciprocals. $\frac{2}{3} \times \frac{3}{2} = \frac{6}{6} = 1$

rectangle a quadrilateral with four right angles and opposite sides parallel and congruent (Lesson 30)

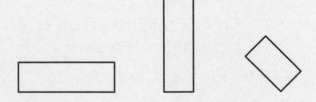

rectangular prism a solid figure with six rectangular faces; opposite faces are congruent and parallel (Lessons 25, 26, 27)

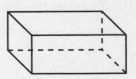

remainder the whole number that is left over when a dividend cannot be divided evenly (Lesson 10)

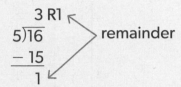

rhombus a parallelogram with four congruent sides (Lesson 30)

round to find which multiple of 10, 100, 1,000, and so on, a given number is closest to (Lesson 8)

9,367 rounded to . . .

the nearest thousand is 9,000

the nearest hundred is 9,400

the nearest ten is 9,370

sequence an ordered list of numbers in a pattern (Lesson 3)

8, 16, 24, 32, 40, . . .

square a rectangle with four congruent sides and four right angles (Lesson 30)

standard form a way of writing numbers using the digits 0 to 9, with each digit having a place value (Lesson 6)

Three thousand, six hundred eleven is written as 3,611 in standard form.

term (in a pattern) a number in a pattern (Lesson 3)

3, 6, 9, 12, . . .

The numbers 3, 6, 9, and 12 are all terms in the pattern.

trapezoid a quadrilateral with only one pair of parallel sides (Lesson 30)

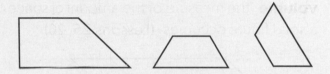

two-dimensional figure a flat figure that only has length and width (Lesson 30)

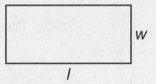

unit cube a cube that has a side length of 1 unit and a volume of 1 cubic unit (Lesson 25)

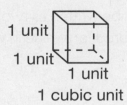

1 cubic unit

unit fraction a fraction that has 1 as a numerator (Lesson 21)

$\frac{1}{3}, \frac{1}{4}, \frac{1}{8}$, and $\frac{1}{12}$ are unit fractions.

unit square a square with side lengths of 1 unit and an area of 1 square unit (Lesson 18)

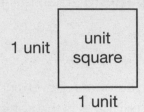

variable a letter or symbol used to represent a number (Lesson 26)

volume the measure of the amount of space a solid figure occupies (Lessons 25, 26)

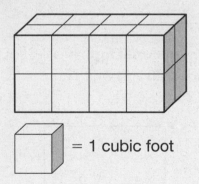

= 1 cubic foot

Volume = 16 cubic feet

word form a way of writing numbers using words (Lesson 6)

2,349 can be written as two thousand, three hundred forty-nine in word form.

x-axis the horizontal number line of a coordinate plane (Lesson 28)

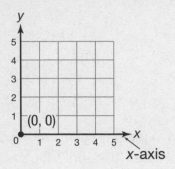

x-coordinate the first number in an ordered pair that tells how many units to move along the x-axis (Lesson 28)

(**2**, 3)

y-axis the vertical number line of a coordinate plane (Lesson 28)

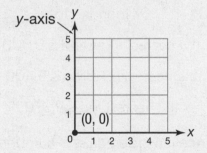

y-coordinate the second number in an ordered pair that tells how many units to move along the y-axis (Lesson 28)

(2, **3**)

Decimal Place-Value Chart

Hundreds	Tens	Ones	Decimal Point	Tenths	Hundredths	Thousandths

Hundreds	Tens	Ones	Decimal Point	Tenths	Hundredths	Thousandths

Grids

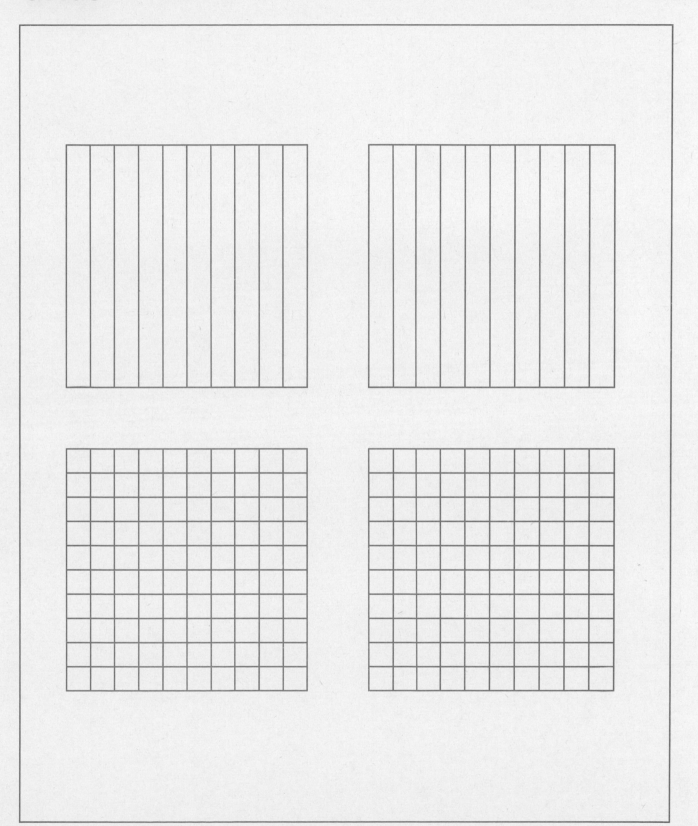

Centimeter Grid Paper

Place-Value Models

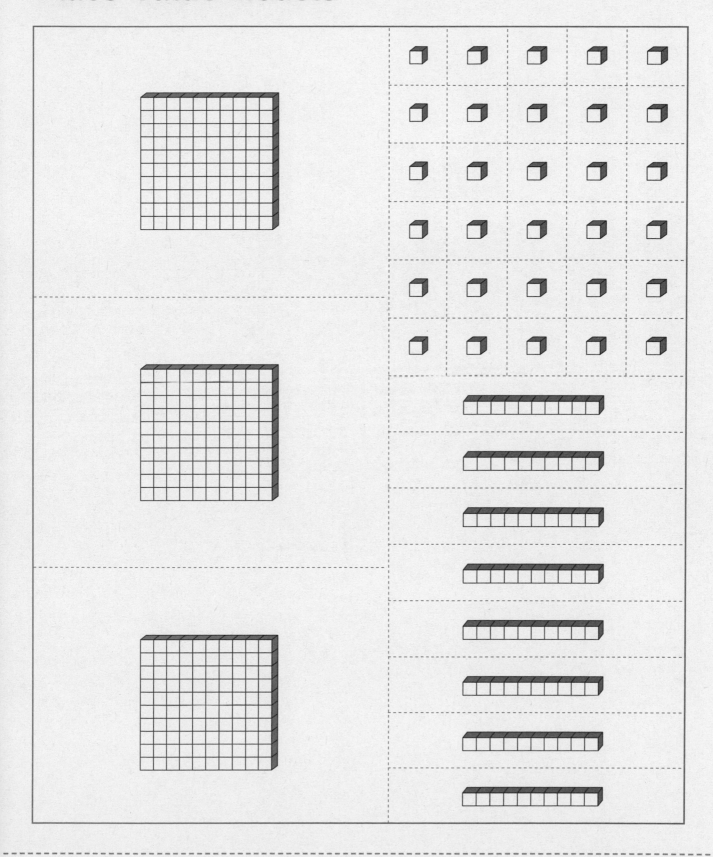

Bills

Grid Paper

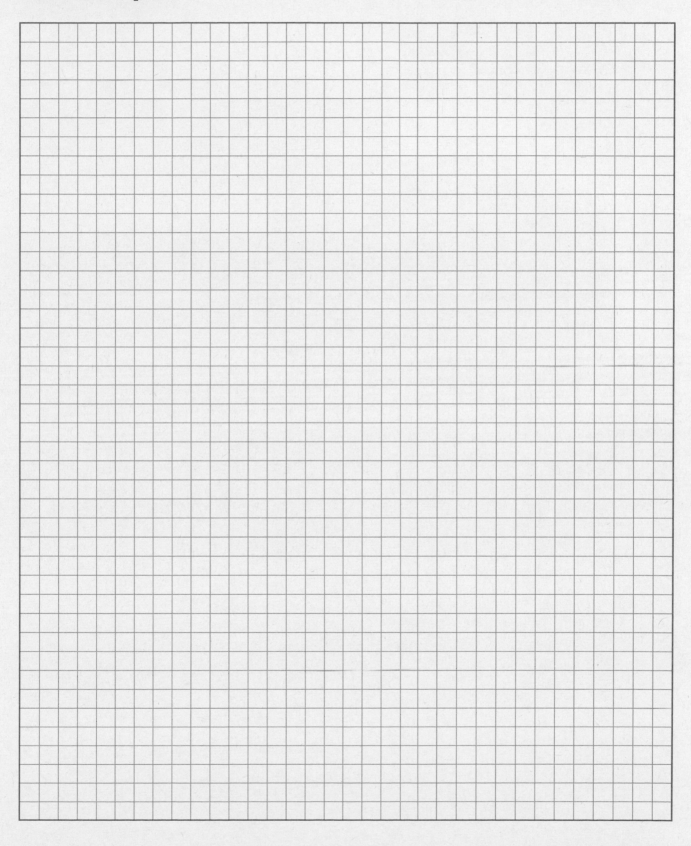

Multiplication Table

×	0	1	2	3	4	5	6	7	8	9	10	11	12
0	0	0	0	0	0	0	0	0	0	0	0	0	0
1	0	1	2	3	4	5	6	7	8	9	10	11	12
2	0	2	4	6	8	10	12	14	16	18	20	22	24
3	0	3	6	9	12	15	18	21	24	27	30	33	36
4	0	4	8	12	16	20	24	28	32	36	40	44	48
5	0	5	10	15	20	25	30	35	40	45	50	55	60
6	0	6	12	18	24	30	36	42	48	54	60	66	72
7	0	7	14	21	28	35	42	49	56	63	70	77	84
8	0	8	16	24	32	40	48	56	64	72	80	88	96
9	0	9	18	27	36	45	54	63	72	81	90	99	108
10	0	10	20	30	40	50	60	70	80	90	100	110	120
11	0	11	22	33	44	55	66	77	88	99	110	121	132
12	0	12	24	36	48	60	72	84	96	108	120	132	144

Fraction Strips

1											

| $\frac{1}{2}$ | | | | | | $\frac{1}{2}$ | | | | | |

| $\frac{1}{3}$ | | | | $\frac{1}{3}$ | | | | $\frac{1}{3}$ | | | |

| $\frac{1}{4}$ | | | $\frac{1}{4}$ | | | $\frac{1}{4}$ | | | $\frac{1}{4}$ | | |

| $\frac{1}{5}$ | | $\frac{1}{5}$ | | $\frac{1}{5}$ | | $\frac{1}{5}$ | | $\frac{1}{5}$ | | | |

| $\frac{1}{6}$ | | $\frac{1}{6}$ | | $\frac{1}{6}$ | | $\frac{1}{6}$ | | $\frac{1}{6}$ | | $\frac{1}{6}$ | |

| $\frac{1}{8}$ | $\frac{1}{8}$ | $\frac{1}{8}$ | $\frac{1}{8}$ | $\frac{1}{8}$ | $\frac{1}{8}$ | $\frac{1}{8}$ | $\frac{1}{8}$ | | | | |

| $\frac{1}{10}$ | $\frac{1}{10}$ | $\frac{1}{10}$ | $\frac{1}{10}$ | $\frac{1}{10}$ | $\frac{1}{10}$ | $\frac{1}{10}$ | $\frac{1}{10}$ | $\frac{1}{10}$ | $\frac{1}{10}$ | | |

| $\frac{1}{12}$ | $\frac{1}{12}$ | $\frac{1}{12}$ | $\frac{1}{12}$ | $\frac{1}{12}$ | $\frac{1}{12}$ | $\frac{1}{12}$ | $\frac{1}{12}$ | $\frac{1}{12}$ | $\frac{1}{12}$ | $\frac{1}{12}$ | $\frac{1}{12}$ |

Unlabeled Fraction Strips

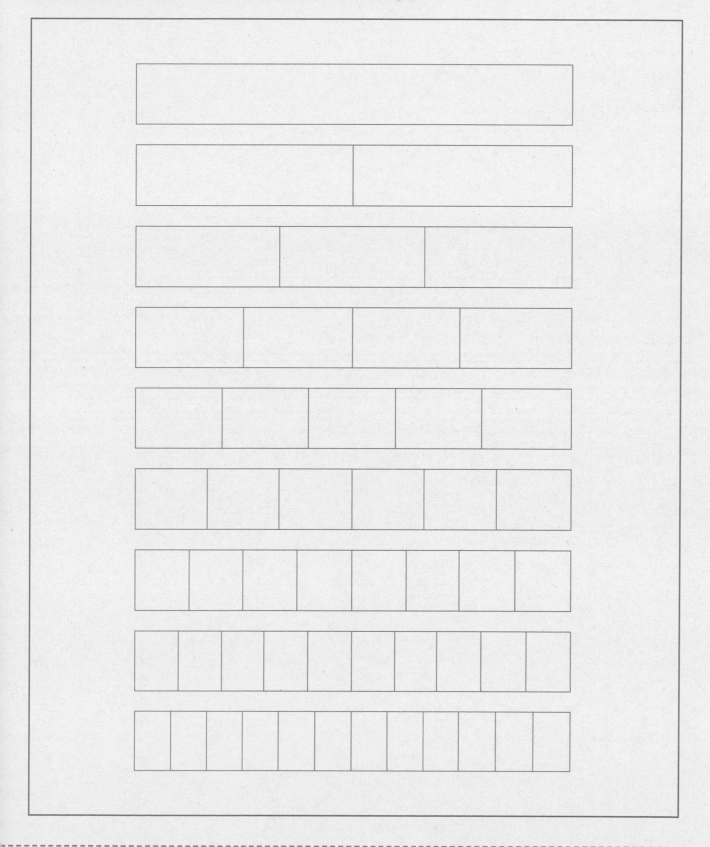

Counters

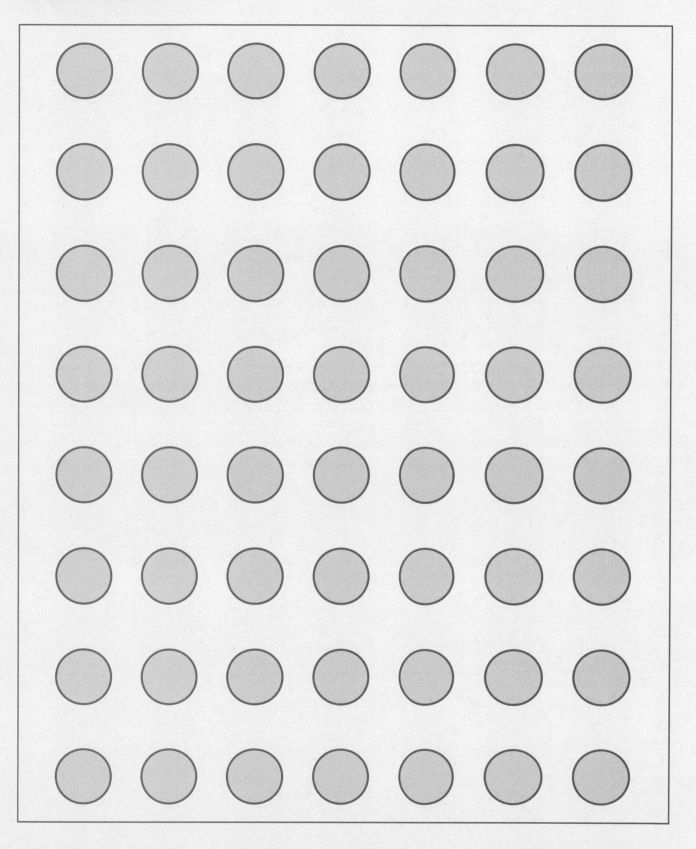

Fraction Models

Fraction Circles

Unit Squares

Customary and Metric Units

Customary Units of Length
1 foot (ft) = 12 inches (in.)
1 yard (yd) = 3 feet (ft)
1 yard (yd) = 36 inches (in.)
1 mile (mi) = 5,280 feet (ft)

Metric Units of Length
1 centimeter (cm) = 10 millimeters (mm)
1 meter (m) = 100 centimeters (cm)
1 kilometer (km) = 1,000 meters (m)

Customary Units of Weight
1 pound (lb) = 16 ounces (oz)
1 ton (T) = 2,000 pounds (lb)

Metric Units of Mass
1 kilogram (kg) = 1,000 grams (g)

Customary Units of Capacity
1 gallon (gal) = 4 quarts (qt)
1 quart (qt) = 2 pints (pt)
1 pint (pt) = 2 cups (c)
1 cup (c) = 8 fluid ounces (fl oz)

Metric Units of Capacity
1 liter (L) = 1,000 milliliters (mL)

Time
1 hour (hr) = 60 minutes (min)
1 minute (min) = 60 seconds (sec)

Number Lines

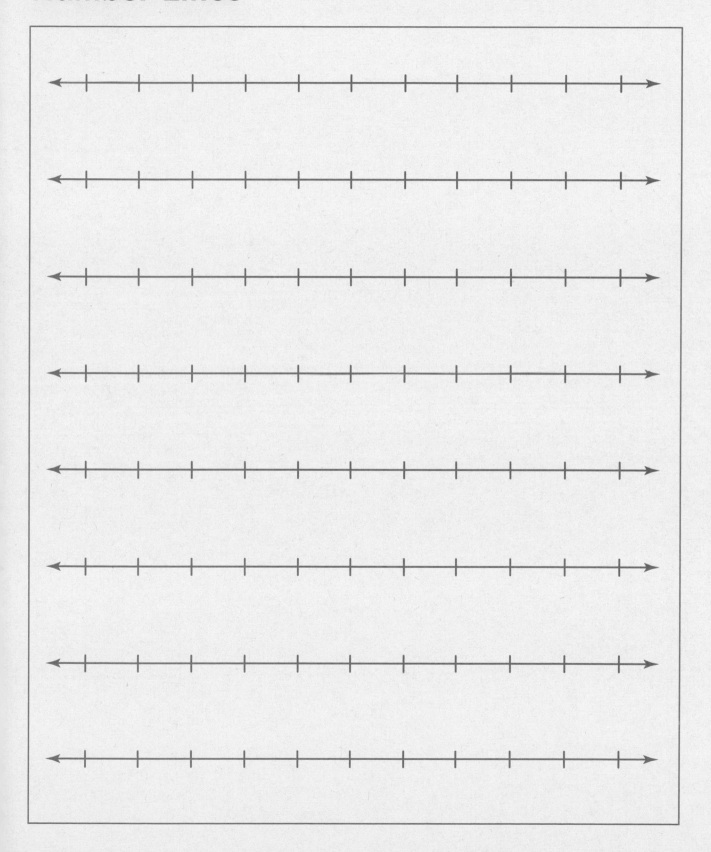

Cubic Units

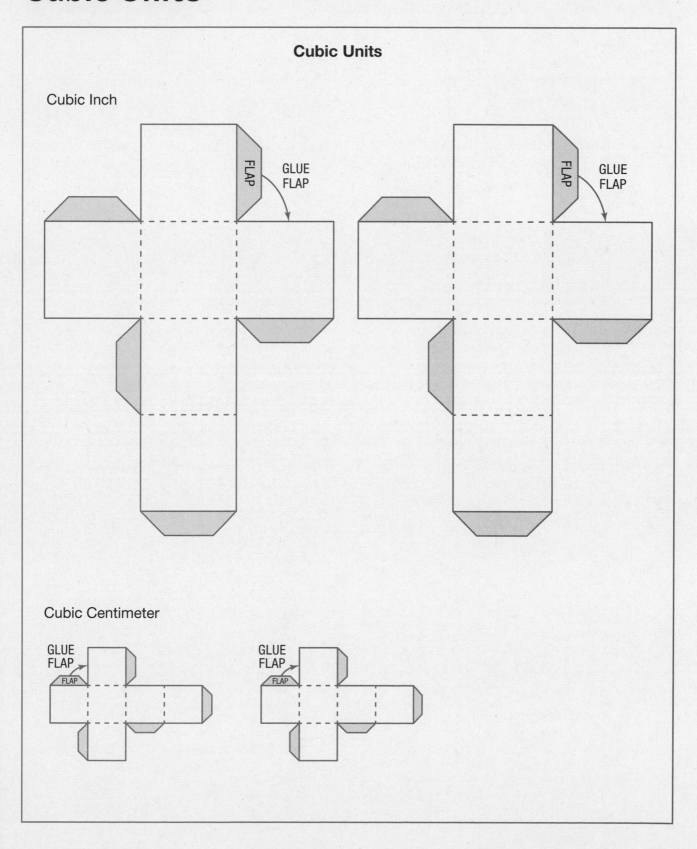

Cubic Units

Cubic Inch

Cubic Centimeter

Rectangular Prism Net

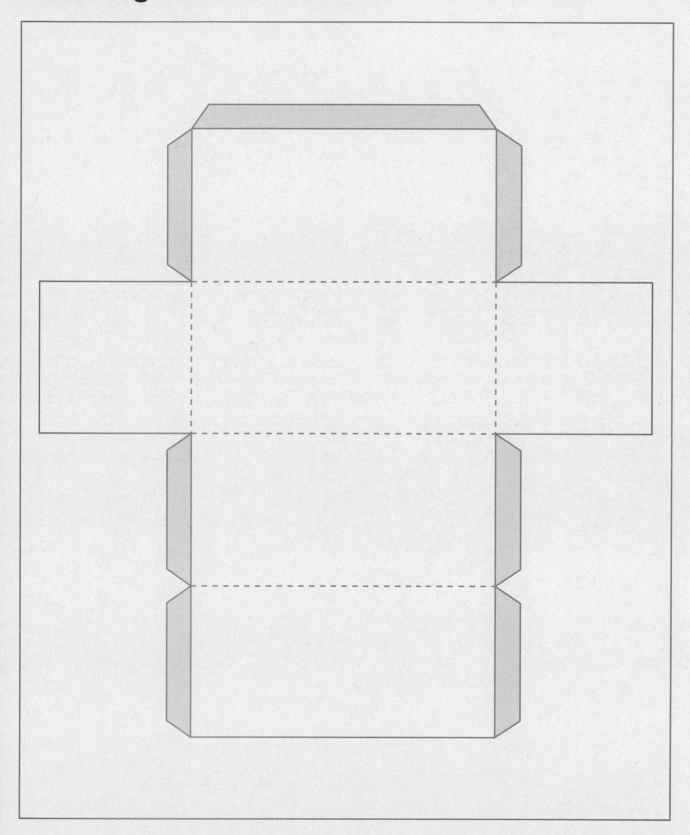

Rectangular Prism Net

Coordinate Grids

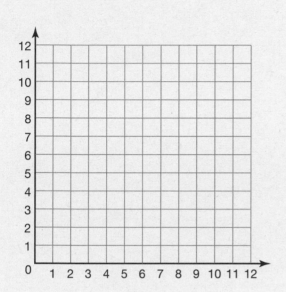

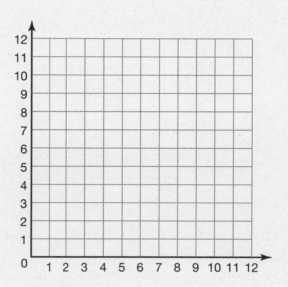

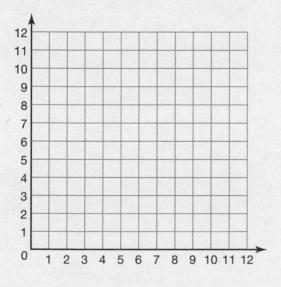

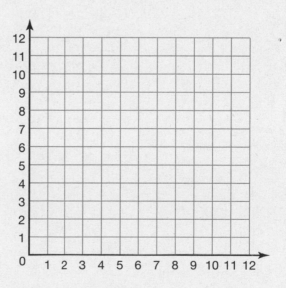

Two-Dimensional Figures

Triangles

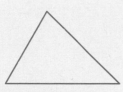

acute triangle
all angles less
than 90°

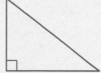

right triangle
one right angle

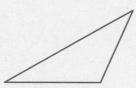

obtuse triangle
one obtuse angle

Quadrilaterals

parallelogram
2 pairs of parallel
and equal, opposite
sides

rectangle
parallelogram with
4 right angles

square
parallelogram with
4 right angles and
4 equal sides

rhombus
parallelogram with
4 equal sides

trapezoid
exactly one pair of
parallel sides

Other Two-Dimensional Figures

pentagon
polygon with
5 sides

hexagon
polygon with
6 sides

octagon
a polygon with
8 sides

Plan the Fair!

Part A

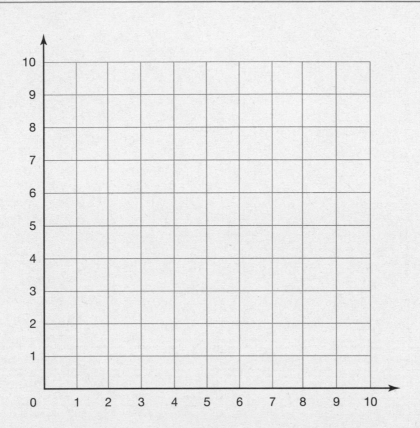

Part B

Activity Spaces	4 Congruent Sides	Exactly 1 Pair of Parallel Sides	2 Pairs of Parallel Sides	4 Right Angles
Fairground			X	X
Petting Zoo				
Entrance				
Games				
Rides				
Stage				
Prizes				